MW00852533

The Story of the Palatines

The Story of the Palatines

An Episode in Colonial History

By
Sanford H. Cobb

New York & London
G. P. Putnam's Sons
The Knickerbocker Press
1897

Copyright, 1897
by
G. P. PUTNAM'S SONS
Entered at Stationers' Hall, London

The Knickerbocker Press, New York

TO THE

CHILDREN OF THE PALATINES

MY

OLD PARISHIONERS

IN THE

HIGH-DUTCH CHURCHES

OF

SCHOHARIE AND SAUGERTIES

PREFATORY NOTE.

M ANY letters, received since the fact became known that the publication of this Story of the Palatines was contemplated, render it proper to state, by way of preface, that the book is purely historical and in no sense genealogical. The sole attempt has been to narrate, in as brief compass as was consistent with the value and interest of the facts, the story of a people. The tracing of the lines of family descent did not come within the scope of such a narrative. To do that for all the Palatines would be work for more than a lifetime ; and were it done, the record thereof would be out of place in a book designed for the general historical student.

Nor has any attempt been made to transfer to these pages the name-lists of the several immigrations. *The Documentary History of*

New York contains the list of those who came in 1708 with Kockerthal, and also some names of those settled at the two Camps. The Pennsylvania Archives contain lists of over thirty thousand names of those who came to Pennsylvania. These lists have been published by Rupp, who also gives names of Palatines on the Hudson in 1711. Beyond these the author does not know of other lists accessible in this country. Nor is he aware that any lists have been preserved in London of the immigrations to North Carolina and Virginia, and of that to New York in 1710. Of this last company Rupp's list of Palatines on the Hudson is a very incomplete record, as many of the people died on the voyage, and many on Governor's Island, while about three hundred settled in the city of New York.

Such lists, however, are not needed for the purpose of this work. The addition of them to the present volume would swell it beyond reasonable limits, and defeat the chief aim of its writing, viz. : the giving to the general student of American history an account, not now widely known, of one distinct and unique element in our colonization, which some historians have entirely ignored and others have treated with undeserved reproach.

The short collection of Palatine names, given in Note I. at the end of the volume, is designed only as a specimen list, taken almost at random, to illustrate the permanency of the Palatine stock, and the changes of form which many of the names have suffered.

S. H. C.

CONTENTS.

CHAPTER   PAGE

I. INTRODUCTION 1

II. THE PALATINATE. 20

III. THE EXODUS 59

IV. THE EXPERIMENT 103

V. THE FAILURE 148

VI. THE PROMISED LAND 201

VII. THE DISPERSION 258

NOTES 305

INDEX 313

MAPS:

I. THE PALATINE OF THE RHINE . . . 20

II. THE PALATINE SETTLEMENTS OF THE HUD-
SON, MOHAWK, AND SCHOHARIE . . 148

III. PALATINE SETTLEMENTS IN PENNSYLVANIA . 258

THE
STORY OF THE PALATINES

CHAPTER I

INTRODUCTION

THE reasons for writing this Story of the Palatines are several. Chief among them are these three: that it has never been written in its fulness, or with proper regard to its historic importance; that much of the little which has been written about it abounds in misunderstandings and misstatements; and that the story truly told is one of such intrinsic interest and bears such relation to colonial history as to make it worthy of regard by every student of American society and institutions.

That which by most people, who know anything about the Palatine Immigration, is supposed to be alluded to in any reference to that
people, is merely the incoming of the large
company which landed in New York in the
early summer of 1710. They made the largest
body of emigrants coming at one time to this
country in the colonial period. There were
nearly three thousand of them, and they were
perhaps at once the most miserable and most
hopeful set of people ever set down upon our
shores.

But they were not all. A small band had
preceded them to New York ; about the same
time as their own coming, a company of seven
hundred had gone to North Carolina, and
another company to Virginia; and in later
years they were followed by many thousands
of their countrymen in the Palatinate, the vast
majority of whom found settlement in Pennsylvania. These various immigrations make
in reality one story, having, as they do, one
source and bound together by a common impulse, constituting a distinct episode in colonial history well worthy of study, and quite
unique in its interest and character.

Of these immigrations there are many scattered notes of mention in Colonial Records, and many incidental and fragmentary allusions in local histories, sketches, and biographies. But of the movement of these people as a whole, with the statement of its causes and the singular experience to which a large portion of them came in America, no full or connected narrative has yet appeared. Much of the brief mention accorded to it is with the evident assumption that the movement was insignificant and possessed of no features worthy of special comment, save the almost unparalleled poverty of the immigration of 1710. The allusions to these people are apt to lay particular emphasis on that condition. They are most frequently called "the poor Palatines." So to some writers they seem to stand in the history as representative only of pauperism, to be dismissed from discussion so soon as possible with scant measure of courtesy or respect. Thus Mrs. Lamb turns them out of court with the following contemptuous paragraph :

"These earlier German settlers were mostly hewers of wood and drawers of water, differing materially from

the class of Germans who have since come among us,
and bearing about the same relation to the English,
Dutch, and French settlers of their time as the Chinese
of to-day bear to the American population on the Pacific
coast."

With this disparaging comment we may contrast the words by which Macaulay describes
the same people :

"Honest, laborious men, who had once been thriving
burghers of Manheim and Heidelberg, or who had
cultivated the vine on the banks of the Neckar and
the Rhine. Their ingenuity and their diligence could
not fail to enrich any land which should afford them an
asylum."

Such contemptuous regard as that of the
language first quoted is surprising to one who
has made even a slight study of the story of
these people, in which are conspicuous other
features than their poverty,—some worthy to
engage the positive interest of every student
of American history, and others fit to compel
the hearty respect of all lovers of truth and
manliness. It is a story of severe and undeserved suffering worthily borne ; a story of the
stubborn and unyielding attitude of men who,

for home and faith, endured an almost un-
equalled fight of afflictions, until at last they
conquered peace, safety, and freedom. As
such, the Story of the Palatines challenges our
sympathy, admiration, and reverence, and is as
well worth the telling as that of any other colonial immigration. We may concede that
their influence on the future development of
the country and its institutions was not equal
to the formative power exerted by some other
contingents. Certainly, they have not left so
many broad and deep marks upon our history
as have the Puritans of New England, and
yet their story is not without definite and permanent monuments of beneficence towards
American life and institutions. At least one
among the very greatest of the safeguards of
American liberty—the Freedom of the Press
—is distinctly traceable to the resolute bold-
ness of a Palatine.

But to create interest in their story it is not
necessary to assert a superiority of influence.
The historian is like the geographer in that
the smaller items, the minor lines and points
of description, claim from him fully as accu-
rate, though not as extended, presentation as

those which are more important.   The coast-
line upon the chart is not complete until it in-
dicates each bay or cove wherein a skiff can
float, and every rock or bar on which a keel
may grate. A river map is not finished which
fails to trace the course of any affluent, though
it be so small that the deer can cross it at a
bound.   The lover of nature looks with different, and yet equal, interest on the little brook,
tumbling riverward down the rocks and be-
neath the forests of the Catskills, and on the
broad bay at the river's mouth, on which the
navies of the world might ride.   Indeed, it is
likely that the beauty of the former will en
chain his eye more strongly than the grandeu;
of the latter.   Certainly, he would deny that,
in order to enlist his regard, the lovely mountain stream must put on the majesty of the
sea. So history finds its pleasing task in
tracing all the streams, both great and small,
which have run together in a nation's life; of
which, while some will challenge admiration
for their volume and lasting power, others will
excite interest by their unique experience, not
to be read without more or less of a sympa-
thetic thrill.

For such reason—whatever may have been
the Palatine influence on our institutions—we
may confidently tell the story of that immigration as something quite worthy of regard. We
may speak of its character, the causes which
gave it rise, the stages of its progress, and the
exceptional experiences of many of these people during their first fifteen years in America,
as making a story quite singular and unlike
any other contained in the history of American
colonization. Very emphatic are the words
of Judge Benton, in his *History of Herkimer
County :*

"The particulars of the immigration of the Palatines
are worthy of extended notice. The events which produced the movement in the heart of an old and polished
European nation to seek a refuge and home on the
western continent, are quite as legitimate a subject of
American history as the oft-repeated relation of the experiences of the Pilgrim Fathers."

There are some general features of this
movement which may be fitly noted here as
suggestive of special interest. The volume of
it was very remarkable. The doors of the
Palatinate seemed to be set open wide, and
through them poured for forty years an almost

continuous stream of emigrants, their faces
set steadfastly towards America. There was
nothing else like it in the colonial period, for
numbers and steadiness of inflow. There were
nearly three thousand of these people in the
company landed in New York in June and
July of 1710. Though the arrivals in port of
the ships bringing them were at intervals
through five weeks, stormy seas having separated the vessels, yet the company was one,
and sailed as such from England under one
command and with one destination. This was
the largest single company of immigrants to
this country until long after the Revolution,
Their number was indeed inconsiderable when
compared with the enormous crowds which
come to America in our day. But at the beginning of the eighteenth century such an influx was notable indeed, giving rise to amaze-
ment and imaginings, and occasion for alarm
to some timorous minds. The community in
city and province was set questioning as to the
meaning of so great an immigration—Whence
came they? Why in so great number, and in
so deep poverty? What could be the object
of the home government in, not only permit-

ting, but encouraging such an influx of foreigners? What shall be done with them? How can they be provided for? The questionings were many. There were grave speculations as to the wisdom of introducing so large a foreign element into these English colonies. When in the following years it was seen that this immigration of 1710 was the prelude to a continuous stream of people from the Palatinate and other parts of the German Empire, this cautiousness found voice in earnest public speech, and sought restrictive power in legislative action. It was loudly declared in some quarters that the unrestricted incoming of alien people, with their strange language and manners, might be dangerous to colonial government and society. Coming in so great numbers and so frequent accessions, they might in a short time obtain the majority in any community, and "subvert our institutions." With the French upon our borders—it was said—always hostile, frequently stirring up the Indians against us, their peace little better than an armed truce, is it wise to admit other aliens to our very firesides?

All this, indeed, did not come to expression

or to thought at once upon the immigration
of 1710, but, most of it, on the continuance of
the movement then begun; which continuance
must be borne in mind in any proper understanding of the Story of the Palatines.   As to
the immediate effect on the colonial mind of
the coming of this first great immigration of
the Palatines, it seems to have been mainly
one of surprise.   In those days travel, by land
or sea, was difficult and with many hardships;
the movement of large bodies of people was
slow; the voyage across the Atlantic took
from three to five months, and was made in
ships devoid of all the comforts which the
modern traveller considers necessities.   The
landing then of this large company was a most
notable thing in the history of the Port of
New York; and to every on-looking New
Yorker, whether Dutch or English, assumed
either the proportions of an invasion or the
dignity of an exodus.

Well—it was an Exodus.   As we study the
story of it, we see that the untaught wonder of
the average on-looker at the time was correct
in its expression.   It was an exodus in the
full sense in which Bible story has taught us

to use that word—a going forth from the
house of bondage to a land of promise. It
was not the incoming of a rabble of distressed
humanity, hurried onward by the mere force
of their misery—objects only for compassion.
It was not a mere company of people deceived
by agents of colonization schemes, and to be
looked upon only as "objects of speculation."
Nor are this people to be considered as merely
moved by that unreasoning unrest which at
times takes possession of the popular mind
with such collective force as to set in motion
migrations and invasions. All of these con-
structions of the Palatine immigration have
severally been suggested and more or less emphasized by those who have alluded to it.

But it is not difficult to show that such con-
ceptions are unworthy and far below the real
dignity of the movement. Attentive regard
will discover in it motives and reasons far
higher than anything which poverty, or unrest,
or speculation can originate. It presents the
impulse, the spirit, the patience, and the hope
which a genuine exodus involves. These men
were men of principle, who had suffered much
for principle and steadfastness therein. The

very poverty, which to some critics seems suggestive only of opprobrium, had come upon
them for such steadfastness. Their story
rightly told must tell of statecraft and church
polity, of the movements and campaigns of
armies. It must speak of sufferings which
approach to martyrdom, of the dark crimes
possible to kings and priests, of the oppressions wrought by unbridled power and the
passive resistance offered by a steadfast ad-
herence to truth. The Pilgrim Fathers were
not the only company who sought in this
western world "Freedom to worship God."
The fact is that, if ever a body of emigrants
came to America from under the hand of the
oppressor, such were these Palatines; and if
ever the thought of religious liberty constrained
men to leave their native land for hoped-for
freedom in America, such hope was powerful
with these children of the Palatinate. Hence
it is, that the story of their coming hither,
with the bitterness and pathos of their an-
tecedent suffering and endurance, and the
sturdiness of their unconquerable faith and
determination to wrest fortune and happiness
out of the very talons of despair, is one that

should be better known to the student of American history.

In addition to that experience of affliction in the Palatinate which was the expelling cause of the migration, there are other elements of the story which give it singular interest and unique place in colonial annals. Perhaps never were a people the objects of such kindly treatment and so lavish generosity as the first few thousands of the Palatines experienced at the hands of the English, the Queen and her subjects vying in the effort to provide for their necessities. That chapter is unexampled elsewhere in history. Equally unexampled in the history of our colonial period is the story of the privation, distress, fraud, and cruel disappointment to which were subjected that large immigration to New York in 1710. Their experience was utterly unlike that of all other bodies of colonists. Those of their countrymen who came in after years, as did emigrants from England or other European countries, met no such distresses, and were under the pleasing compulsion only to subdue the wilderness and make for themselves homes in a new land. But the Palatine

immigrants of 1710 found, to their bitter sorrow, that they had only made an exchange of
masters. For fifteen years they suffered, with
a disappointment of their hopes, a continuance
of affliction; they were cheated and oppressed,
and became the helpless victims of vindictive
and rapacious men. Much of their affliction
in America is set down by some writers to
their own ignorance and obstinacy. But it
will appear that their ignorance was rather an
unwise trust in the promises of those in power,
and that without their obstinacy, which in Europe had maintained their faith, they never, in
that generation at least, would have found in
America security of home and freedom. This,
to the average reader, will seem a strange
statement as descriptive of any community
in the colonial period. Of that period, the
most prominent conception is of an era in
which the oppressed of the Old World found
without failure an unrestrained freedom on
American shores. For the most part this conception is true; and it is the unlikeness of this
description to the early fate of these Palatines in New York which makes their experience during the first decade and a half

so remarkable an episode in the history of the colonies.

As to the permanent influence of this Palatine immigration, it goes without the saying that it were impossible for such sturdiness of stock, such patient and firm persistence in the right, such capacity for endurance, and such buoyancy of hope, conjoined with such addiction to religion, to be absorbed into American life without a deep impress on the character of after generations. Nor does the historian wait long for its testimony. Solely on account of the large influx of this German, and chiefly Palatine, element into Pennsylvania, bringing thither their qualities of industry, thrift, steadiness, and piety, the contemporary historian, Mortimer, declared that "Pennsylvania is since become by far the most populous and flourishing colony for its standing of any in British America."* So early did the beneficial effects of this immigration begin to manifest themselves.

And to this day we can see with small effort the reproduction in the population of the Keystone State of that same moral earnestness,

* *History of England*, iii., 233.

soberness of mind, and unflinching persistence which composed the "staying" qualities of the early Palatines.

In like manner a similar monument is left in New York, in many towns in the Hudson and Mohawk valleys, and on the banks of the beautiful Schoharie, wherein are found many names of the early migration, families in direct descent and with the same old High Dutch leaven, delighting in memories of the fathers, steadily ambitious to emulate their virtues, thrifty, industrious, intelligent, and godly. Out of this stock came many who were second to none in the ardor of the Revolution. Far better than most of the people of the colonies they knew what it was to suffer under the hand of the oppressor, and by contrast how desirable were the blessings of liberty. Whole companies of them went to the front,—brave and loyal always,—first against the French and Indians, and afterwards against the British. They were largely Palatines whom Herkimer led to the battle of Oriskany, "of all the battles of the Revolution, the most obstinate and murderous."* It was to the Americans

* Fiske's *Am. Revolution*, i., 292.

a technical defeat, indeed, but one of those
defeats which rival victories; for it shattered
the plans of the British campaign, sent St.
Leger with his regulars and Indians back to
Oswego, and delivered Burgoyne into the
hands of Gates.

Herkimer, than whom no braver man fought
in the War for Independence, was the son of
a Palatine immigrant, and lends his glory to
their story.   Other names might be cited in
the same category of Palatine extraction and
honorable public service.   A stock that produced such virile and widely serviceable characters as Weiser, Herkimer, Heister, and the
Muhlenbergs,—of which last name no less
than four of those who bore it have laid
America under tribute for praise and honor,
—such a stock should not be considered the
least significant or influential among those
which have made our country what it is.

These then are the reasons for telling
this Story of the Palatines.   We would rescue it from undeserved obloquy.   The tale
will take us far afield.   We have not only to
look at that miserable company—sick, dis-
couraged, sordid in their poverty and deci-

2

mated by disease—landing at New York in
the summer of 1710. We have to inquire
what thrust them into that evil case. We will
need to visit the land which they and their
followers spurned with migrating foot. We
must see them ground between the upper and
nether millstones of kingcraft and priestcraft.
We will have to follow the tracks of armies,
and listen to some of the contentions of royal
cabinets. Then across the sea in the new
land we shall note their various settlements
and dispersion.

The sources of information on many points
are far from full, leaving many gaps in the
narrative which the reader wishes to have
filled. Yet comparison of the accessible data
makes it possible to construct a tale, which we
do not hesitate to publish as the true Story of
the Palatines, and which is confidently offered
as a thing of interest and value to the student
of American history.

It is probable that many more items of the
story might be found in the papers of the
Lords of Trade, preserved in London, and in
other archives of the English Government.
But the labor and expense of consulting them

do not seem demanded by the task in hand.
All the main facts and much of the minute detail are accessible in this country.   It will be
seen from the list of authorities cited, that no
small pains have been bestowed to arrive at a
true understanding of the facts, and to place
this Episode in its deserved position among
the records of our colonial times.*

* See Note III.

CHAPTER II.

THE PALATINATE.

THE name of the Palatinate, as that of a political division, disappeared from the map of Europe before the opening of the present century, the principality being finally shattered by the Napoleonic wars. From the thirteenth century to the close of the eighteenth it maintained a varying importance among the continental powers. Its boundaries were changeable with the shifting fortunes of diplomacy and war. Situated between the greater and rival powers of France and the German princes, its soil was the frequent path of armies and field of battle. Either of the greater combatants, but more frequently the French, was wont to appropriate what towns and castles, what broad acres and treasures of the Palatinate he thought himself able

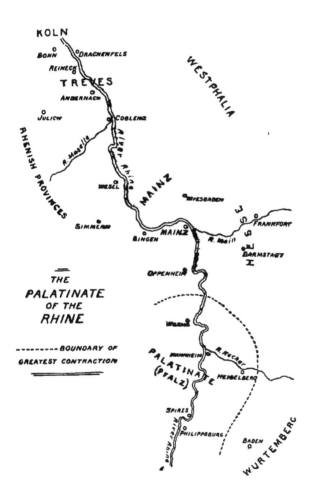

KOLN

BONN   DRACHENFELS

REINECG

TREVES

AMBERNACH

JULICW   COBLENZ

WESTPHALIA

RHENISH PROVINCES

R. Moselle

River Rhine

WESEL

MAINZ

WIESBADEN

SIMMERN

BINGEN   MAINZ

FRANKFORT

R. Main

DARMSTADT

OPPENHEIM

THE
PALATINATE
OF THE
RHINE

-------- BOUNDARY OF
GREATEST CONTRACTION

WORMS

PALATINATE
(PFALZ)

MANNHEIM   R. Necker

HEIDELBERG

SPIRES

PHILIPPSBURG   BADEN

River Rhine

WURTEMBERC

to retain. In the settlement of treaties, however, when each contestant was wearied by the war, and when, more often than otherwise, the *status quo* was re-established—proof of the folly of the war—the reigning prince of the Palatinate was apt to come to his own again.

There were, in fact, two Palatinates—distinguished as the Upper, or Bavarian, Palatinate, and the Lower, or Palatinate of the Rhine—or the Pfalz. The latter, with which alone this story is concerned, was by far the more important, and so overshadowed the other that, when the name Palatinate was used without qualifying word, the understanding was of the Rhenish province. Its boundaries may be somewhat vaguely stated as the states of Mainz, Treves, Lorraine, Alsace, Baden, and Wurtemberg; boundaries subject to more or less of expansion and contraction, according as one or other of its little provinces became the spoil of war. Its lands lay on both sides of the Rhine, extending from near Cologne above Mannheim and containing somewhat less than 3500 square miles. Its capital was Heidelberg and its principal cities were Mayence, Spires, Mannheim, and Worms, all of which, with still others, have obtained famous place in history.

The origin of the name, Palatinate is notable. Derived from the title of its ruler, it means the principality of the Palatine. This title, Palatine, is in itself peculiar, and receives its explanation from imperial institution. It is supposed by some writers to go so far back as to imperial Rome and to the Palatine Hill, with its palace of the Cæsars.* Others date the title from the time of the Merovingian kings of France, with whose court was connected a high judicial officer, called *comes palatii.* He was Master of the royal household, " and had supreme authority in all causes which came by fiction to the king. When the sovereign wished to confer peculiar favor upon the holder of any fief under him, he granted him the right to exercise the same power in his province as the Comes Palatii exercised in the royal palace. With this function went the title *Comes Palatinus,* Count Palatine, and from the ruler the province received its name."

Butler † gives a somewhat broader explana-

* Appleton's *Am. Cyc.*
† *Revolutions in Germany,* Proofs and Illustrations, p. 45.

tion of the title, as one conferred by the Emperor in the Middle Ages upon those who in his name administered justice to the empire. Evidently the original intention of the officer was with the idea of a High Court of Justice. As such the title is even found in English history, conferred by both William I. and Henry II. on nobles in the centre and west of England. As an English title it soon passed away, but retained its place for centuries upon the Continent. Under the old Hungarian constitution it was the title of the royal lieutenant, who at a later period officiated as mediator between the nation and the sovereign, and as President in the upper house of the Diet. Also in Poland the title obtained for the governors of the larger divisions of the kingdom. None of these ever achieved as Count Palatine, any historical prominence. The chief significance of the title is found in the story of the Palatinate, the ruler of which was a king in everything but name, and frequently exercised large influence on European politics.

Now, the curious thing in historical nomenclature is that, unlike all other princes, the ruler of the Palatinate did not receive his title from the land he governed, but from his title gave the name to his dominions. Louis XIV., with all his magnificence, took his title from his realm and was known as King of France. But the Count Palatine was not so named because he ruled the Palatinate, but that country was the Palatinate because its ruler was a Palatine. Another curious thing is that the people of the Palatinate were described by the same name as their prince. They were all Palatines together, a title with him descriptive of place, honor, and authority, but with them only of birth and nationality. Such, indeed, is the fact with respect to all the emigrants from that country, though how widely the name may have obtained in continental usage does not appear. It is somewhat curious that these people should at times be called Palatinates—a misnomer which is almost grotesque. It is the same sort of absurdity as though one, in speaking of Englishmen, should call them Englands. Palatinate is the name of the country and never properly used for its inhabitants, who are always to be called Palatines, with their princes. As a name for the American immigrants, indeed, it had obtained such vogue, doubtless in consequence of the impression made on the colonial mind by the character and volume of the early immigration of that people, that for many years all Germans coming to this country, whether from the Palatinate or other provinces of the Fatherland, were called Palatines.

At the first the title of Count Palatine signified only a personal office, expiring with the life of its possessor, and to be renewed only on the pleasure of the Emperor in such person as his favor should designate. Probably under such conditions, and with such limitation of tenure, the title may have been more widely conferred as special and personal mark of imperial regard. In many such cases it must have been a title more of honor than of authority. This personal and temporary character certainly obtained with the Palatines of England, Hungary, and Poland. As early as the twelfth century, however, the title of the Palatines of the Rhine became hereditary, and no longer dependent on the favor of the Emperor. Until near the end of the thirteenth century the Palatines of the Rhine were the Dukes of Bavaria, the last of whom to bear both digni-

ties was Louis, the Severe.   He died in 1294,
leaving two sons, Louis and Rudolph, between
whom he divided his dominions.*   Louis, the
elder, took the more important and became
Duke of Bavaria, while his brother received
the Palatinate, and founded what is called the
Rudolphine line of the Palatine family.   The
position of the Palatine was in all respects
regal, save in so far as it was limited by those
loose bands which bound all the German
States, together with Austria, in the Holy
Roman Empire.   During the tenure of the
Rudolphine line, the dignity and power of the
Palatine were further increased by the imperial gift of the Electorship.   By reason of this
gift in rank and position, the title of the prince
was changed, who thereafter was no longer
Count, but the Elector, Palatine.

The Rudolphine house became extinct on
the death of Otho, the twelfth of the line, who
died without issue in the year 1559.   On his
death the Palatinate passed to Frederick, of
the house of Simmeren—or Zimmern—who
became the founder of the so-called Middle
Line of the Palatines.   The accession of Fred-

* Butler's *Revolutions in Germany.*

erick, in addition to the change of dynasty, marked an epoch of importance in the history of the Palatinate, in that he associated himself and his house with the Reformed, or Calvinistic, branch of the Protestant Church.

The Zimmern line ended with the death of the childless Charles in 1685, and gave place to the related House of Neuburg in the person of Philip William. Philip died in 1690, and was succeeded by his son John William, whose reign as Elector Palatine lasted until 1716. It was in his reign that the Palatines of our story began their exodus, and it was from his hand that proceeded the last and most immediate, though not the greatest, impulse to that emigration.

This impulse, it may be said in passing, was religious, for, while this emigration was not from under a pitiless and destructive persecution for religion's sake, and while it may be doubted whether so large an exodus of this people would have taken place had their religion only have come in question, yet it is beyond denial that among the strong incentives which led them forth was the desire for religious liberty, free from the vexing and oppress-

ive interference of capricious monarchs. The
religious history of the Palatinate, so far as
concerns the attitude and measures of the
government, was indeed capricious. The situation of the country brought the people into
early contact with the Reformation and its
great teachers. Wittenberg was not far to the
east, and Geneva no farther on the south, and
the people were open-eared to both Luther
and Calvin. For some years before the court
of the Elector Palatine had pronounced its
adhesion to the Protestant faith the principles
of the Reformation had taken almost universal
possession of the people. Both Lutheran and
Reformed doctrine found a friendly and fertile
soil in the Palatinate. The numerical strength
was with the followers of Geneva, to that extent that for generations the Palatinate was
known as a stronghold of the Reformed;
while the Lutheran element, found in large
numbers, was accorded by their neighbors of
the Reformed faith the charity and tolerance
of a common Christian brotherhood. So when
the people began to flock across the sea,
Lutheran and Reformed came together, bringing each his own special thought and desire of

worship and doctrine. It is interesting to note in the history of their settlements in America, that almost in every place where they made their permanent homes both forms of the Protestant faith found early foothold and habitation. Side by side they erected their humble churches, since grown in many places into noble temples. And to this day, in the valleys of the Hudson, the Mohawk, the Schoharie, and the Swatara, the children of those Palatines, still Lutheran and Reformed, worship side by side as their fathers of the sixth generation gone worshipped on the Rhine.

But of this unity in difference the rulers of the Palatinate can not be exhibited with their people as examples. They lagged behind the people in breaking the bond of the Roman faith, and it was not until 1546 that Frederick II., the then reigning Elector Palatine, gave in adhesion to the Protestant cause—especially espousing the Lutheran faith. As already noted, Frederick III., the first Palatine of the House of Zimmern, signalized his accession to power by the strenuous advocacy of the Reformed doctrine. During his reign, on his urgency and authority, Olevian and Ursinus,

professors of divinity in the University of
Heidelberg, published that Catechism, which
under the name of Heidelberg remains to this
day throughout the various branches of the
Reformed Church, the dearest among its sym-
bolical books ; and is also recognized throughout the Protestant world as the best and
choicest of the Creeds to which the Reformation era gave rise ; specially notable, at once,
for its freedom from the controversial spirit of
the age, and for the high tone of spiritual experience which it depicts.

The successors of Frederick III. did not all
adhere to the Reformed doctrine and Church,
but with a vacillation, not recorded of other
rulers of their century, exhibited a change in
the religion of the Palatine and his court on
nearly every accession to the throne. A Calvinist in the Electorship was pretty certain to
be followed by a Lutheran, who in his turn
gave place at death to another Calvinist, to be
followed by yet another Lutheran. It was a
kind of religious seesaw, in which all the power
of royal favor and influence of court patronage,
and at times the force of decrees and enact-
ments, were thrown now at one end of the

beam and soon again at the other, to the no
small confusion of the people, and in many
instances to their very serious discomfiture and
loss. For in those days throughout Christendom obtained the old motto, "*Cujus regio, ejus
religio*"—(whose is the country, his is the religion ;—or, the religion of the prince, must be
that of his people). This as an axiom had
come down from the time of Augustine, who
defined the first duty of the State "to buttress
the invisible City of God"; and of all the
great minds of the Reformation period the only
one to break away from its dictum was the
Stadtholder of Holland, William the Silent.
Luther and Calvin, Knox and Cranmer, and
even the Puritans of New England acknowledged as vital the principle that the State
could interfere in the religion of the subject.
Not only did they assent to the axiom as correct, but they incorporated it in their confes-
sions and institutions. It took not only the
persecutions of Papal Rome, the Holy Office
and the sword of Alva ; but also the innumerable petty persecutions of Protestant against
Protestant, to teach the world the meaning and
divine right of religious liberty. Nor could

the Old World furnish a fitting field for its demonstration.   There was needed the free soil of
the America, to which that band of Palatines
came, before this greatest of all human rights
could find expression in national life and law.
And it may be added, this definition and enact-
ment of Religious Liberty is as yet the great
gift of America to the world ; which liberty in
its purest form—strange as it seems at this end
of the nineteenth century—among all the great
nations of Christendom exists alone in America
to-day.

It is not then a matter for surprise that the
people of the Palatinate should suffer many distresses under the sway of varying religionists,
though all were of the Protestant faith.   Each
successor in the throne endeavored to change
back again, in the interest of either Lutheranism or Calvinism, what his immediate predecessor had recast to his own mind.   The story
of the Reformation tells of no other such religious kaleidoscope, turning over and over to
the constant unsettlement of the public comfort.   When, in 1690, John William became
the Elector Palatine, he brought on the greatest change of all, seeking not to turn his peo-

ple from one to other Protestant communion, but to reverse the action of Frederick II., and bring the Palatinate again under the Roman See. He was a man of saturnine disposition, devotedly attached to the Roman Church, and needing only the power of Philip II. of Spain to rival his reputation as bigot and persecutor. Under his rule the poor people of the Palatinate suffered in their religious affections and privileges far more than the variable Protestantism of his predecessors had inflicted. To him Lutheran and Reformed were alike obnoxious, and in all ways possible he signified his intention to bring back his dominions to their ancient faith. To the people already suffering from the intolerable hardships which the cruelest of wars had thrust upon them, this persecuting spirit of their prince came as the last impulse to break off their attachment to the fatherland and send them to make new homes in distant America.

Of the wars which wrought upon the Palatines so piteously and expulsively, it falls in place to make brief note. There were two of them, covering almost the entire period between the years 1684 and 1713, with but

3

four years of so-called peace thrust into the
midst of it. The first is known as the war of
the Grand Alliance, and the other as that of
the Spanish Succession. Of the former the
conquest of the Palatinate was the exciting
cause, while in the latter, though the integrity
of the Palatinate was not again at stake, its
poor people became again the prey of a brutal
soldiery. Both wars were due to the over-
weening ambition and rapacity of Louis XIV.*
The possession of the Palatinate had long
been the object of his most covetous desire.
Like all the princes of France, and almost all
Frenchmen from the time of Philip Augustus
to our own day, Louis considered that the
frontier of France could be properly constructed
only by the left bank of the Rhine. For this
object many battles have been fought and
many thousands of men have died. To the
mind of France one of the chief glories of
Napoleon was that he gave to her that
boundary, and to-day the deep grudge of
France against the German is that, twenty-
five years ago he wrested from her the
Rhenish provinces. So to Louis, the modern

* Menzel's *History of Germany*, ii., 498.

Ahab, through the first half of his long reign,
the fertile meadows and vine-clad hills of the
Palatinate, its populous towns and many castles
with the smiling river in the midst, made a
Naboth's vineyard which of all things he
desired to call his own. Thus incited he made
miserable the lives of the two Electors Palatine, Charles Louis and Charles, by every
deceitful art of diplomacy and by many violent
raids into their dominions. With the hope of
propitiating him Charles Louis, in 1671, gave
his daughter Elizabeth Charlotte in marriage
to Philip of Orleans, the brother of the French
king. But there, as in almost every other
instance in history, the bond of kinship proved
but as a rope of sand against the demands of
an aggressive policy of state. The insolence
of Louis hardly received a check. The lights
had hardly been extinguished upon the nuptial
banquet, when Turenne led an army into the
Palatinate to ravage the west bank of the
Rhine. This was in 1674, and in the following years the policy of Louis so repeated his
harassments and insults that the proud spirit
of the Elector Palatine, Charles Louis, at
last gave way, and he died "of a broken

heart" in 1680.   His son Charles, subjected
to like treatment by Louis, had but a short
reign, dying childless in 1685.

With the death of Charles what Louis
counted his great opportunity had come.   The
bonds of family alliance, which were too weak
for restraint from insolence and oppression,
seemed quite strong enough for the transfer-
ence of a principality.   He denied the right
of Philip William of Neuburg to the succession, and demanded the Palatinate for his
brother Philip, in right of his wife, the sister
of the dead Palatine.   The demand roused
all the German princes in opposition.   The
League of Augsburg was formed against Louis,
embracing Bavaria and all the German States,
and under its protection Philip William assumed the Electorate Palatine.

Meanwhile, two other great events provided
strength and bitterness for the coming conflict.
In the autumn of 1685 Louis, incited thereto
by the persuasions of Madame de Maintenon,
revoked the Edict of Nantes, by which Henry
IV. had given safety to the Huguenots and
eighty years of prosperity to France.   At once
began the flight of the Refugees—"best blood

of France "—to seek safety and new homes in
other lands. Many of them found a warm
welcome with the Palatine and his people,
against whom, for this act of harborage, the
wrath of Louis " smoked like a furnace."
Holland and England had also opened their
doors to the fugitives, but the Palatinate
especially, for the double reason that it was
more accessible and was itself the object of
his long desire, became the victim of his
anger.

In addition to this element of the quarrel
another was given by the deposition of James
II. from the throne of England in 1688, and
the accession of William of Orange. James
was received with royal honors at Versailles,
established in state at St. Germain, and made
a pensioner on the bounty of Louis, who both
refused to acknowledge William and aided
James in his futile efforts to recover his lost
crown. This precipitated the angry action
of the English king and parliament. England
with Holland joined the League against France,
and its name was changed to the Grand Alliance.

The war raged for nine years, and in the

Palatinate with unparalleled ferocity.   Louis,
anticipating the action of the allies, sent 50,-
000 men into the Palatinate under General
Montclas.   History accredits to Madame de
Maintenon an insatiable rage against the Palatine and his people for the asylum afforded to
the Huguenots, and to her intrigues and persuasions that Louvois urged upon the king,
that "the Palatinate should be made a desert."
Macaulay dissents from this condemnation of
Louis's wife and represents that she expos-
tulated with the king against this policy of
rapine, and that, having in vain interceded for
many cities, she at last secured the saving of
Treves.   Possibly this view may be correct.
The responsibility of de Maintenon for the
banishment of the Huguenots is, however,
beyond question, but one can take pleasure in
thinking of this as the effect of pure religious
bigotry unmixed with any love of cruelty.
Nor, indeed, is it necessary to consider Louis
as overpersuaded to that atrocity by his wife,
or any one.   The experience of vast and irre-
sponsible power had long since made him a
stranger to either pity or remorse.   Neither his
judgment nor his will approved the Revocation

of the Edict of Nantes. He was too wise in king-craft not to perceive the great material damage to the kingdom involved therein. To this he was overpersuaded by his wife and her priests. But having yielded to their solicitations and committed himself to their policy of extermination, he needed no other incentive than his own vindictiveness. Partly in revenge for the Protestant welcome given to his banished subjects, partly in anger at not securing the Palatinate for himself, and partly to render the country unfit for occupancy by the allies, he gave such orders as must have fully satisfied the utmost passion. Montclas and his lieutenant, Melac, were neither unwilling nor slow to execute the orders of Louis with as literal and complete a fulfilment as possible. Melac boasted that "he would fight for his king against all the powers of heaven * and of hell." Says Macaulay † :

"The French commander announced to nearly one half-million of human beings that he granted them three days of grace, and that within that time they must shift for themselves. Soon the roads and fields which then lay deep in snow were blackened by innumerable men,

* Menzel, ii., 499.　　† *History of England*, iii., 123.

women, and children flying from their homes. Many
died of cold and hunger, but enough survived to fill the
streets of all the cities of Europe with lean and squalid
beggars, who had once been thriving farmers and shop-
keepers."

Every great city on the Rhine, above Cologne,
was taken and sacked. Worms, Spires, Andernach, Kuckheim, Kreuznach, were laid in ashes.
The fortress of Philippsberg was completely
destroyed. Villages without number were
given to the flames. The Elector Philip, look-
ing from the walls of Mannheim counted, in
one day, no less than twenty-three towns and
villages in flames. Heidelberg suffered to some
extent, but its castle escaped for a few years
only the violence which in 1692 made it the
most picturesque ruin in Europe. Many of
the unoffending inhabitants were butchered.
Many were carried into France and compelled
to recant. In Spires the brutal soldiery, as
though to express their contempt for things
most sacred, broke open the imperial vaults
and scattered the ashes of the emperors. The
whole valley of the Rhine, on both its banks,
from Drachenfels to Philippsberg, was made
the prey of the demon of rapine and destruc-

tion. The crumbling walls, the deserted castles fallen into ruin, the isolated towers, ivy
covered, which to-day interest the traveller on
the Rhine, giving associations of historic
beauty to almost every hill washed by its waters, are the marks, as yet indelible, of the
wrath of Louis and the rapacity of his army.
These ruins still remain, softened and beau-
tified by time, but they tell a tale of fearful
atrocity. And, in reality, far worse than aught
they witness to, was the unspeakable barbarity
suffered by the people. In the midst of the
destruction of the towns and villages, such of
the poor villagers as endeavored to rescue their
goods were slain. " Everywhere in the fields
were found the corpses of wretched people
frozen to death. The citizens of Mannheim,
were compelled to assist in destroying their
fortifications, and then driven out, hungry and
naked, into the winter cold, while their city
was burned. In the neighborhood of Treves,
Cologne and Julich the peasants were forced
in the following summer to plow down their
own standing crops." * The French, having thus wrought in the Palatinate and the

* Lewis's *History of Germany*, p. 462.

small States in the north, passed on through
Wurtemberg and Bavaria, on all roads with
fire and sword.   At the end of the campaign,
" a list of twelve hundred cities and villages,
that still remained to be burned, was exhibited
by these brigands." *

In 1689 Louis attempted through Jacobite
intrigues the assassination of William III., and
this outrage, added to the ferocities of the previous year's campaign in the Palatinate and
Bavaria, at last aroused the hitherto indifferent
Emperor Leopold, who now made common
cause with the petty princes of Germany, who
were in danger of being trodden under foot by
the despotic monarch of France.†   He procured the "decree of the Diet of Ratisbon
(1689) which expelled every French agent
from Germany and prohibited the employment
of French servants and any intercourse with
France ; the Emperor adding these words,
'because France is to be regarded not only as
the empire's most inveterate foe, but as that
of the whole of Christendom, nay, as even
worse than the Turk.'"   This added new

* Menzel's *History of Germany*, ii., 500.
† Menzel, ii., 501.

fury to the war and new suffering to the poor
people. In 1692 the French again turned
attention to the Palatinate, as though to pick up
what they had left behind four years before,
and seizing Heidelberg, blew up its famous ·
castle, leaving it the ruin that it is to-day.
Thence through the valley of the Neckar and
the higher Rhine, they resumed the destructive measures of the past.

The war with varying fortunes drew out its
fearful length to 1697, with the balance of gain
and by far the most brilliant victories on the
side of Louis. But it was impossible of continuance. The finances of Louis were nearly
exhausted, and a new ambition was luring him
in view of the near death of the childless King
of Spain. Meanwhile, the mutual distrust of the
Allies was weakening their strength, and both
parties to the contest hastened to conclude the
Peace of Ryswick in 1697. This Peace makes a
bitter satire on the utter folly of the war. By its
terms Louis restored all his conquests to their
legitimate possessors and recognized William
of Orange as King of England. " Thus terminated," says Labberton * "this vast war, in

* Labberton's *Historical Atlas*, p. 135.

which the two parties had displayed on land and sea forces incomparably greater than Europe had ever seen before in motion. France, in order to maintain herself against this coalition, had nearly doubled her military status since the war with Holland. The result had been a barren honor. Alone against all Europe she had contrived to conquer, but without increasing her power. For the first time, on the contrary, since the accession of Richelieu, she had lost ground." In the midst of the war the Elector Palatine, Philip William died, in 1690. His son and successor, John William, as already noted, was a devoted adherent of the Church of Rome, and at once, while his people were still smarting under the terrible sufferings of the war, set himself to compel their conversion to his own faith. Bishop Burnet describes him * as "being bigoted to a high degree." He gives also an interesting sketch of Herr Zeiher, the representative of the Elector Palatine at the Congress of Ryswick, as † "born a Protestant, a subject of the Palatinate, he was employed by the Elector Charles Louis to negotiate affairs

* Burnet s *History of His Own Times*. iii., 223.
† *Ibid.*, iv., 63.

at the court of Vienna. He, seeing a prospect of rising at that court, changed his religion and became a creature of the Jesuits. He
managed the secret practice with the French
in the treaty of Ryswick by which the Protestants of the Palatinate suffered so considerable
a prejudice." "The Elector Palatine," says
Menzel,* "instantly enforced the maxim,
Cujus regio ejus religio, throughout his dominions, and simulated Louis XIV. in tyranny
towards the Protestants, who emigrated in ·
large numbers."

The peace instituted by the treaty of Ryswick had but short life. Scarcely had the soldier put off his harness when he was summoned
to put it on again. Another and greater war
followed quickly on that of the Grand Alliance,
once more making all Europe a camp and once
more bringing desolation upon the people of
the Palatinate. This was the war of the Spanish Succession, the origin and objects of which
may be stated in few words.

Charles II. of Spain, the last of the Haps-
burg dynasty, died without issue in 1700. The
decision as to the succession had for years be-

* *History of Germany,* ii., 503.

fore his death furnished large occupation to the
cabinets of Europe. There were three claimants : the Dauphin, the Emperor Leopold, and
the Electoral Prince of Bavaria, a grandson to
the Emperor and as yet a child. Among these
claimants the Spanish people indicated no preference, only insisting that the empire should
remain undivided. It is not necessary for us
to detail the grounds on which the conflicting
claims were based. Suffice it to say, that
Charles, in his will, declared the young Bavarian Prince the heir to all his dominions, hoping by such devise to forestall and prevent the
impending conflict. Had the young Prince
lived, it is possible that he might have ascended the Spanish throne without serious
opposition, and the fearful war have been
averted. But his sudden death in 1699, while
Charles still hovered over the grave, opened
the question afresh and made the war inevitable. The agents of Louis at once beset
Charles, to extort from his weak mind an indication of favor towards the French claim. To
these efforts was added the powerful influence
of the Papal Embassy. Thus they succeeded
in obtaining from the moribund monarch an-

other will, by which he set aside the renuncia-
tions of the two Infantas, mother and wife of
Louis, and devised the crown of the entire
Spanish Empire to Philip of Anjou, the grand-
son of Louis. At once, on the death of Charles,
Philip assumed the crown, under the title of
Philip V., and all Europe sprang to arms.
Austria, Prussia, Bavaria, and the smaller
German States formed a coalition against
France; and again, as in the preceding war,
Louis added to the number of his enemies by
insolence to England. The disposition of
William and his parliament was to keep out
of the contest; only stipulating that, though
the reigning houses of both France and Spain
might be Bourbon, the two crowns must never
be united upon the one head. But this passive attitude of England was suddenly changed
into fury by an uncalled-for insult from Louis.
While the opposing forces of the Continent
were as yet only preparing for the conflict, the
exiled James died at St. Germain, September,
1701 ; and Louis acknowledged his son as King
of England. It is difficult to account for such
action, save on the ground of sheer malicious-
ness, for Louis was too astute a statesman to

suppose that the son of James could ever as-
cend the English throne. It was as though,
having had William for a foe in almost all his
wars of the past, he could not regard the new
lists properly drawn without his old enemy in
his front again. If this were his motive, he
succeeded to perfection. Not only William,
but all England was thoroughly roused, and
decided to take part with the coalition. William, beyond all comparison the master statesman of Europe, was all powerful in Holland.
That sturdy nation, always fighting on William's side, whether Stadtholder or King, went
with England into the alliance, and again presented the spectacle of France fighting single-
handed against all the great Powers. The war
lasted twelve years, being terminated in 1713
by the Peace of Utrecht. In this war the
great victories were on the side of the allies.
Blenheim, Ramillies, and Oudenarde set the
names of Marlborough and Eugene among
the greatest of the world's generals. It is a
curious contrast presented by this war and the
preceding with regard to their results. In the
former all the great victories were won by
the armies of Louis, but he kept nothing of

all gained thereby. In the latter Louis was defeated in every great battle, and yet he won what he fought for,—the crown of Spain for his grandson. By the treaty of Utrecht Philip was confirmed in its possession, though the empire was dismembered. The only other power to gain anything of permanent value in the war was England. She, in 1704, obtained possession of Gibraltar, as yet, nearly two hundred years after, unwrested from her grasp. The heaviest fighting of the war was in Bavaria, Northern Italy, and the Netherlands; but the Palatinate came in for its full share of accustomed desolations. It would seem that Louis could never forgive his failure to steal the principality for himself. His armies, seeking their foes in the north and east, made broad swathes of destruction across the Palatinate, notwithstanding the favor of the Palatine for the French and his religious sympathy with Louis. In every year one or other portion of the little State was made to suffer from the brutality of the French; and in 1707 the Marshal Villars led into it an army with the intent to repeat the work of desolation wrought by Montclas in 1688, having the same, though

4

not so universal, result in burning towns and impoverished people. And then began that exodus which brought so many thousands of the poor people to America.

At the first glance it may seem needless to relate, even after so brief fashion, the foregoing story of the two wars, which made for the subjects of the Palatine such a furnace of affliction. But it is well to see all things in their historical perspective. The cause of the lowliest, the sufferings of the humblest, gain in dignity—and that worthily—from association which groups them with the great events of history. This thought alone were sufficient for setting the emigration of the Palatines in its proper place as related to the councils of princes and the movement of great wars. This would be sufficient in telling any tale of historical interest.

But, as hinted in the Introduction, there is special reason for dwelling upon the influences of war and religious oppression as furnishing the moving causes of this migration. For some reason not explained the usual understanding has been quite different. In England, in the year after the migration of 1710, when

The Palatinate 51

the tide of sympathy and charity had ebbed
which sent the Palatines on their hopeful way
to America, and when the Tories had dis-
placed the Whigs from power, a committee of
the House of Commons appointed to investi-
gate the causes of the Palatine emigration,*
reported that it was entirely due to land
speculators, who had obtained patents in the
colonies and had sent agents into Germany to
induce the peasantry to emigrate to America
upon the said lands. Stress is laid upon the
fact that the Palatines themselves had acknowledged the receipt of papers and books containing the portrait of Queen Anne, urging
their emigration and promising gifts of land.
No mention is made in that report of any other
influence leading to the emigration, and the
inference is made that these poor Palatines
were deluded "objects of speculation," whom
the arts of the land agents had, for their own
purposes, foisted on the British public, to the
great disturbance of home and colonial affairs.
This report, evidently biased by political feeling and by disgust at the continuance of
appeals for aid to the emigrants, cites the

* Burnet's *Own Times*, iv., 258.

Naturalization Act of 1708 as among the chief of the evil instruments that had precipitated on English shores this great stream of people from the Palatinate.

Some modern writers, who have alluded to the subject, seem to have been content to take this report as completely disposing of the question, and quenching the title of these Palatines to historic sympathy. It is remarkable that so scholarly a man as Dr. Homes, formerly Librarian of the State of New York, should have accepted the conclusions of this report as justified by the facts in the case.* He intimates that not much credit should be given to the Palatine claim that this people became exiles because of oppression.

One can hardly fail, on full study of the question, to be surprised at such conclusion ; for while it may be true that agents did solicit the migration, this fact is entirely consistent with the other fact that, because of sufferings endured through war and religious persecution, this people became promising objects of such solicitation. That is to say—the agents of land companies, if such there were,

* *Trans. Albany Institute*, vii., 106-132.

supposedly shrewd and businesslike, saw in
the down-trodden and oppressed people of the
Palatinate a field of operation, because of their
very afflictions.   While with an eye only to
business they addressed their propositions to
the poor Palatines, the solicitations must have
seemed to open " in the valley of Achor a
door of hope."

⌐ It is notable also that, not only in 1708 and
1709 were all these emigrants departing from
the Palatinate, and equally oppressed Swabia
on its southern border, but also for forty years
after, the vast majority of German immigrants
to America were from the same quarter.   The
question is evident: Why should the land agents
have confined their efforts to the Palatinate,
and the Palatines alone have been desirous of
emigration, unless there had been in their condition, and in the disposition of the government under which they lived, causes of such
grave moment as predisposed them to leave
their country ?   The singularity of choice by
the agents of the Palatinate alone, and the
ready disposition of the people to listen to
their offers, as well as the remarkable fact that
they alone of the Germans of their day had a

desire to change their country, certainly demand a broader and more significant explanation than a speculative fever.   But given the
condition of destitution resulting from the
French invasion and the harassing measures
of a Prince filled with proselyting zeal, we see
at once the combination that disposed the
people to at once accept the opportunity of
escape.

It is significant also that, while the Palatines
in London frankly stated the fact that they
had been urged by the agents to their migration, yet in all their formal statements, petitions, and addresses to the authorities in
England and America they cite the cruelties
suffered from the French as the great cause
of all.   Some of their statements also affirm the
religious oppression in their own country as
another powerful influence toward emigration.

It is to be noted that Burnet, while record-
ing the action of the House of Commons and
the report of its committee, does not indicate
his own judgment as in accord with its conclusions.   On the contrary, in the two passages
already cited,* he appears to state his own

* Burnet's *Own Times*, iii., 223. iv., 63.

opinion that the Protestant people of the Palatinate were subjected to no small prejudice and distress by the oppressive measures of John William.

Further, Dr. Homes, in the article above noted, objects that the claim of the Palatines that the cruelties of the French had driven them from their country, is not to be credited, because the ruthless campaign by which Louis desolated the Palatinate was in 1688, twenty years before the exodus began. Were this the only campaign in which the French soldiers had ridden rough-shod over the fields and villages of the Palatinate, the objection certainly would hold good. Twenty years surely were many enough to smooth out the roughnesses so caused and to reclaim the ravaged land. But, while that campaign was undoubtedly the severest under which that devoted land suffered, yet others followed. Again and again, through the years of the war of the Grand Alliance, the armies of Louis swept through the country, and, although not staying to wreak deliberate and wide-spread ruin, yet left want and suffering on their trail. A like ill fortune fell upon the principality with the

opening of the War of the Succession, cul-
minating in the deliberate invasion of Villars in
1707 to emulate the rapine of Montclas and
Melac. It is strange that Dr. Homes should
have overlooked these facts. They import an
amount of suffering entailed upon the poor
people of the Palatinate not easy of estimation, and certainly both great and immediate
enough to justify their statement, that they
left their country in consequence of the cruelties of the French. And it is very significant
that the first outward movement was immediately subsequent on the invasion of Villars
in 1707. That was the last burden which,
added to all the loss and suffering of the past,
set on foot the emigrating thousands ; first to
Holland, then to England, and finally across
the sea.

Still another item of disproof of the judgment that this emigration was solely due to
the agents of the American Proprietaries is
found in the fact, that they had made no provision for the care and direction of the emigrants, either in transit or after reaching
America. The only apparent exception to
this statement is the existence of a committee

of assistance at Rotterdam, through whose
offices the Palatines were helped *en route*, and
so speedily as possible shipped to England.
But there is no evidence that this committee
was instituted by agents of the Proprietaries,
and it may have had its origin from the authorities of Holland, in the same manner as it
became a necessity for the English authorities
to provide in some way for this great body of
strangers. This seems the most reasonable
supposition, for had there been anything like
a concerted movement of the Proprietaries or
Patentees in America to promote emigration to
their lands, it seems impossible that they could
have failed to provide some measures by
which the scheme could be effected. Of this,
however, there was absolutely nothing. The
agents, if any such there were, disappear at
once that the migration, supposed to have
been excited by them, is begun. The thousands flocking from the Palatinate are thrown
naked upon England, to be cared for and directed at the expense of the government and
of public charity. It was impossible for agents
to lay their calculation for such an issue as is
found in the unparalleled benevolence of the

British people towards these poor Palatines.
We will have to conclude, that, while sundry
so-called agents may have found access to the
Palatinate, they really represented no business
enterprise and undertook none such ; and that
the people, learning of the avenue of escape
from their accumulated wrongs, needed for
their emigration no other inducement.

CHAPTER III.

THE EXODUS.

THE first formal note of the emigration, as already begun, is found in a report of the British Lords of Trade.* No record exists of the starting of the people from their homes upon the Rhine, as of the inception of a great enterprise. Indeed, this were impossible. With whatever of undertone of concert of action the movement was set on foot, its beginnings in the Palatinate had to be in quietness and stealth. The Elector Palatine was of a mind to lose none of his subjects, and made vigorous protests against their emigration. Among other deterrents he published an edict threatening death to all who should attempt to emigrate from his dominions. So, of necessity, the departure of the emigrants,

* *Doc. Hist. of N. Y.*, iii., 327.

if not "by night," was unheralded. In fact for years there had been a steady though small stream of the afflicted people seeking quieter countries. Northern Germany and Holland had received thousands of them. And now that the thoughts of the refugees were turned westward, they found countrymen in the cities of Holland to help them on their journey.

It is probable that we should cite, as the first contingent from the Palatinate to America, a small band which, after much toil and disaster, · found settlement in New Jersey. There is but small record of this company, and how much of their story is due to local tradition can hardly be decided.* The tale is of a company of Lutherans who, in 1705, fled from persecution at Wolfenbuttel and Halberstadt. They went into Holland, and thence, in 1707, embarked for New York. By stress of storm their vessel was driven to the south, and after tedious delays found harbor at Philadelphia. Being still determined to go to New York, the little company set out to reach that city overland, and had nearly accomplished their journey

* *Penna. Mag. of Hist.*, x., 376. *Story of an Old Farm,* by Mellick. Introd.

when, attracted by the beauty and fertility of
the region they were traversing, they resolved
to go no farther. They had reached the edge
of the Schooley's Mountain range, and look-
ing off upon the land, now in the borders of
Morris County, they decided that no more desirable place of habitation could be found. So
there they settled. Happily for them, neither
the crown nor the provincial government
seems to have been concerned about them.
They were left unmolested to build their homes
and beget a posterity still visible in many well-
known families of that region.

The more formal pioneers of the emigrating
movement were a company of forty-one who
came to London in the spring of 1708, and ·
applied to the Board of Trade to be sent to
America. The Report, alluded to above, has
reference to this application, and bears date of
April 28, 1708. It takes the form of a Memorial to the Queen, in which the Lords
comment on a Petition from the Rev. Joshua
Kockerthal, an Evangelical minister, on behalf
of himself and other

"poor Lutherans, come hither from the Lower Palatinate, praying to be transferred to some of your Majesty's

plantations in America ; in number 41, viz : 10 men, 10 women, and 21 children ; in the utmost want, being reduced to this miserable condition by the ravages committed by the French when they lost all they had."

The Board notes the testimonials of good character brought by the company, and on the question of their location sets aside the West Indies, on account of the hot climate, and proposes "to settle them on Hudson's River, where they can be made useful in the production of Naval Stores and as a Frontier against the French and Indians." It is further recommended that "they be transported in the Man-of-War and Transport ship to go with Lord Lovelace," who had been recently appointed to the governorship of New York ; that they "should be supplied here [London] with necessary tools for agriculture, and must be supported for awhile by the Queen's bounty, or by the Province, and before departure should be made Denizens of this Kingdom." It is further intimated that, if the Queen would confirm the provincial act annulling certain extravagant patents granted by Governor Fletcher, she would be able to grant the usual number of acres to these poor Palatines. The suggestions of the Lords of Trade were approved by the Queen in Council, and order was taken on 10 May, 1708, for the naturalization of the Palatines and sending them to New York with Lord Lovelace.

Meanwhile, before this company was embarked, another petition from Kockerthal represents that fourteen others had joined him and his company,* three of whom were from Holstein. He describes this company as " in a Deplorable Condition, having suffered under the Calamity which hap'ned last year in the Palatinate by the invasion of the French," and prays that they may receive from the Queen the same kind treatment given to the first company, and be with them sent to America. This petition, which bears date of June, 1708, was granted by the Queen, and the fourteen Palatines were made denizens of the kingdom.

In this petition Kockerthal also asks, in view of his clerical profession, that he be given a " Sallary, inasmuch as he cannot hope for a competent subsistence in America." To this no attention is paid by the authorities, and, on the 7th July, Kockerthal addresses another

* *Colonial Hist. of N. Y.*, v., 44.

petition,* again asking for a salary and for £20 towards an outfit. To this the Lords of Trade advise the Queen, that no precedent exists for granting stipends to foreign clergymen in the colonies—only that the French minister in New York receives annually £20 or £30, " but by what order we do not find." The Board, however, in consideration that Kockerthal is poor, suggests that the sum desired for outfit be granted to him, and as his people are poor, he be given a glebe of 500 acres, with liberty to sell some of it for his immediate maintenance after reaching America.

These two companies were undoubtedly one in the scheme of emigration ; for some cause becoming separated on the way to England, whence, being reunited, they went together across the sea. It is interesting to note that in the company were thirteen families and two unmarried men. All the names, even of the children—some of which names are still worthily represented by their descendants †—are on record. All were Lutherans in religion ; and as to occupations, the majority of the men

* *Col. Hist.*, v., 62. *Doc. Hist.* iii., 328.
† See Note I.

were farmers, one was a clergyman (Kockerthal), one a weaver, one a stocking-maker, one
a blacksmith, one a carpenter, and one a clerk.
The composition of the little emigration has
the aspect of an enterprise well planned for the
settling of a new community in strange scenes.
It would seem also that some concert must
have existed between this company and their
countrymen left behind. They went out as a
band of pioneers, or prospectors, to see what .
might be the promise of other lords and a new
land ; and it is altogether probable that their
report sent home of the kind treatment received by them from the English authorities,
will go far to account for the large influx of
the Palatines to England in the following year.
This probability becomes almost a certainty
from the fact—of which only an incidental note
is found in the epitaph on Kockerthal's tomb-
stone—that, having settled this first company
in America, he returned at once to England,
and came out again with the large emigration
of 1710, which accompanied Gov. Hunter. Of
this larger emigration it will fall to speak presently ; but for the moment it will be more
convenient to trace the fortunes of this first
5

company, which were quite distinct from those
of their following countrymen.

Kockerthal and his companions sailed with
· Lord Lovelace in the autumn of 1708, arrived
in New York in the following winter, and so
soon as possible were settled in the district
then known as Quassaick Creek and Thankskamir.* This district is part of the territory
of the present city of Newburgh, the name of
which may be a monument of this settlement
by the Palatines, whose prince was of the House
of Neuburg. The region round about on the
west side of the Hudson had been purchased
from the Indians by Gov. Dongan in 1684.
In 1694 it had been conveyed by patent to
Capt. John Evans by Gov. Fletcher, but four
years later this patent, together with others in
the province, was annulled by the legislative
Council of New York. The lands were afterwards parcelled out in smaller grants, the first
of which, after much delay, was given in 1719
to the Palatines, under the name of the German Patent. This patent covered 2190 acres,
which lay along the Quassaick, or Quassey,
now called Chambers Creek, touching the

* Ruttenber's *Hist. of Orange Co.*, p. 245.

Hudson and stretching up the side of the steep hills.

Shortly after their arrival, Lord Lovelace, who had been especially charged with their care and oversight, died in New York, and the Palatines very soon began to suffer want. In the fall of 1709 they represent, by petition to Lt. Gov. Ingoldsby, that the promised sustenance had not been given to them,* and appeal to the compassion of the Governor and Council. When this petition came before the Council, it was there stated that nineteen of the Palatines had abandoned their Lutheran faith and had become Pietists ; and the Council ordered that only the rest should be supported. An inquiring committee, however, soon reported that no such religious troubles existed and that the entire community were entitled to the promised subsistence. Order was thereupon taken to " victuall " all, and to distribute "clothes, tools, and other necessities—such as building materials, iron and steel, books, paper and medicines, horses, cows and pigs." The trouble for the provincial authorities in the matter was, that they had entered into no

* *Doc. Hist.*, iii., 329.

obligations to subsist these people, who were stipendiaries of the home government and the Crown.   Nor was the Council willing to saddle their support upon the treasury of the province.   At the same time they were unwilling that the poor people should perish almost before their very eyes.   They intimated their willingness to afford subsistence, if any " Gentlemen can be found " to guarantee repayment by the government.   The Palatines—to whom arrears are still in default—report to the Council, in October, 1709, that they have found such security in the persons of Col. Nicholas Bayard and Octavius Conradus, and pray for the much needed relief.   The language of their petition, which is signed by John Conrad Codweis, is quaint and naive enough to deserve an extract.   It presents " most humble prayers to your Honours' Generosity, to let descend Your tender Commiseration towards the precarious and miserable circumstances of this poor people, wherein they certainly shall perish this Winter, if not speedily supplied, and thus render all past outlay of the Government useless."   This touching plea wins the compassionate action of the Council, which orders the desired aid, only stipulating that the Palatines themselves shall repay the advance, "if England refuses, in a year!" Within the year Gov. Hunter arrived in New York, with the first and only advance of the British government for the subsistence of the Palatines in this country, and it may be taken for granted that the Council, who allowed to escape few opportunities for harassing that long-suffering "Brigadeer," lost no time in presenting their bill.

In the year 1713 the Governor directed the Surveyor-General * to lay out for the Palatines the land which, six years after, was constituted the German Patent, specifying that tracts should be allotted "for each of them his quantity distinctly." Forty acres were to be reserved for highways and five hundred for a Glebe, and the whole was to be known and called "The Palatine Parish by Quassaick."

At this time Kockerthal, who had returned from England with Hunter and the immigration of 1710, was already established at Quassaick. He probably brought with him to Quassaick a small number of that large com-

* Ruttenber, p. 248.

pany, though the great majority were settled
at the two Camps, fifty miles farther up the
river. Over the people in all the Hudson
settlements Kockerthal exercised very considerable authority, partly on account of his min-
isterial office, but more largely because of the
native strength of his character. He was evidently a shrewd man, far-seeing and careful,
able on a wider field, if such had been given
to him, to be a noted leader of men. His influence with his countrymen in America was
supreme. They looked up to him with no
little reverence, and the provincial authorities
had often to appeal to his influence in the en-
tanglements, which almost immediately began
in the settlements of East and West Camp.
Probably having his longer residence at Quassaick, he took the pastoral care, not only of
the people in that place, but also of those in
the settlements above. Himself a Lutheran,
he seems to have maintained the most harmo-
nious relations with that portion of the people
who were of the Reformed faith, among whom
labored a certain John Fred. Hager, one of
the emigration, who afterwards carried his
missionary efforts into the Mohawk and Scho-

harie valleys, and to Pennsylvania. Kockerthal organized a Lutheran church at the Camp
on the west bank of the Hudson, and probably had some part in the similar organization
on the opposite side of the river. Both
churches are still existent and among the dozen
oldest ecclesiastical organizations on the continent. Kockerthal died in 1719 at West
Camp and was there buried. His grave, until recently, was marked by a stone, bearing
a quaint inscription in German, of which the
following is an English translation : *

" Know, wanderer, under this stone rests, beside his
Sybilla Charlotte, a right wanderer, the Joshua of the
High Dutch in North America, the pure Lutheran
preacher of them on the East and West sides of the
Hudson River. His first arrival was with Lord Lovelace in 1707-8, the 1st January. His second with Col.
Hunter, 1710, the 14 June. His voyage back to England was prevented [lit., interrupted] by the voyage of
his soul to Heaven on St. John's Day, 1719.

" Do you wish to know more ? Seek in Melancthon's
fatherland, who was Kockerthal, who Herschias, who
Winchenbach ?

" B. Berkenmayer, S. Huestin, L. Brevoort, 1742."

The names Herschias and Winchenbach

* *Mag. of Am. History*, 1871, p. 15, article by Rev. J. B. Thompson, D.D.

are said by local tradition to be those of Kockerthal's sons-in-law. The last three names are probably, as Dr. Thompson suggests, those of the men who, twenty-three years after the death of Kockerthal, erected the stone. Within the year just past this stone was removed from the grave and placed as a mural tablet in the interior of the church of West Camp.

After the death of Kockerthal the story of the Quassaick Parish presents but few notes of interest, and the most of these have regard to the affairs of the church. From that time the parish had no pastor of its own, but was ministered to on semi-annual, or annual visits by the Lutheran clergyman of New York, who for some years was to receive the profits of the Glebe. The members at Quassaick were received into the New York church, to which church they loaned the bell given to them by Queen Anne, to be returned whenever the people at Quassaick should be able to erect a house of worship. That house was afterwards built, in 1733, and was still standing until within the memory of some of the oldest citizens, and known by them as "the Glebe School House." It is pleasant to know that the bell

was returned, and also to note the hint suggested of the long-headedness of Kockerthal,
who, before leading his first colony over the
sea, sought and obtained from the royal favor
this bell, which was to wait more than twenty
years for its destined place.

What may have been the after fortune of the
bell is not recorded, but for the most of the
Palatines at Quassaick it soon ceased to utter
its Sabbath summons. The majority of the
people were not satisfied with their location.
They found the stony hillsides more unyielding of produce than they had hoped, and lis-
tened with envious ears to the tale of more
fertile farms to be had in Pennsylvania, whither
many of the settlers at the Camps and Schoharie
had migrated. A large proportion of them,
after not long debate, sold their farms upon
the Quassaick, and departed to join their com- ·
patriots in the valleys of the Swatara and Tulpehocken. The sale of these farms brought
many of them, indeed the most of them, into
the possession of others than Palatines, who
were called by the original settlers, "Dutch
and English new-comers." With these began
the influx of immigrants of other stocks, an in-

coming promoted by Governor Colden, whose
son Alexander had large holdings in the neighborhood, with the result that in a short time
the few remaining Palatines were very largely
outnumbered by the Dutch, Scotch, and English.   It was but a natural issue that the direction of vicinage and church affairs should soon
pass from the hands of the Palatines.   Men of
English blood were chosen in Parish Meeting
as Trustees of the Glebe and Church, and steps
were at once taken to bring the Church into
connection with the Church of England.   This
. took place in 1743 and thereupon the " Palatine Parish by Quassaick " ceased to exist,
though it was not until 1751 that the Glebe
was finally turned over by Letters-Patent to
the Church of England.

And this must end our story of the Newburgh Palatines, the majority of whom had
sought other and distant homes.   But they left
behind them a sturdy stock who, though soon
absorbed into the general life of the non-
Palatine community, have left monuments of
their worth.   Themselves and their descendants—not a few of whom have to-day, in the
fair city of Newburgh, names on the roll of

Kockerthal's companions—were "not a whit behind" the men of other stock in the expression of solidity of character, intellectual alertness, love of freedom, and moral worth,—equal factors in building up the civil and religious institutions of their city and State.

We turn now to the far more extensive migration which, in the year after the departure of Kockerthal and his first company from the country of the Rhine, followed them to England. Of this movement, as of its precursor, no records are extant, or accessible, detailing its organization and departure from the Palatinate. Among the influences helping the decision to emigrate at that time, Conrad Weiser—himself one of the emigrants and twelve years of age at the time—in an autobiography written in his old age instances the severities of the winter of 1708-9. "Birds perished on the wing, beasts in their lairs, and mortals fell dead in the way." *

The first mention of the exodus as begun is in the recorded presence of the Palatines in London in surprising numbers, to the no small astonishment of the English people and the

* *Life of Conrad Weiser.*

equal perplexity and embarrassment of the
authorities. The migration was evidently a
concerted one at home, with lines stretching
into all parts of the principality. The impression made by it at Rotterdam and London
was such as would be caused by the irruption
of an entire tribe. Weiser has a fine bit of
fervid description. " A migrating epidemic
seized on the stricken people, and, as a wave,
thirty thousand Germans washed along the
shores of England. Israel was not more as-
tounded at the armored carcasses of the Egyp-
tians lying by the banks of the Red Sea, than
were the people of England at this immense
slide of humanity."

Both for charity's sake and in their own
defence, the people of Rotterdam speeded
them over the channel into England and to
London, where their swarming numbers put to
the proof, not only the ingenuity of the government to devise their future destination, but
also its ability to provide for their pressing
and immediate needs.* They began to arrive
in London in May of 1709, and by the end of
June their numbers amounted to five thousand.

* *Trans. Alb. Ins.*, 1871, p. 106.

Before August was passed this number was nearly doubled, while thirteen thousand is set as the aggregate by the end of October. In the London of to-day such an influx would be little more than a drop in the bucket; and yet, even to-day, were a horde of thirteen thousand men, women, and children to suddenly throng its streets, most of them without a penny to pay for food or lodging, many of them in rags and tatters, there might be furnished something of perplexity in finding a solution to the problem of their immediate care. In the London of two hundred years ago the facilities for caring for the traveller and the stranger were of the crudest and most limited description. Those who could pay their way must put up with many discomforts in the inns, which were few and of small capacity. The city was entirely unprovided with ready means to meet the demands thus suddenly made by the flocking Palatines, who, pouring in such crowds upon London, threw themselves upon the generosity of the English government and people. They seemed to say : " Here we are. What are you going to do for us ? What are you going to do with us ? "

It is difficult to imagine the state of perplexity which at the first must have filled the
official mind. In the past it had not been
accustomed to deal with such problems, or to
concern itself about the poverty or destruction
of the poor. But this problem was so great
and the appeal of the Palatines so strident,
that a hearing ear and active hand were compelled. The impression made upon all the
English was profound, and the interest in this
great company of refugees was felt, far beyond
the limits of the capital, in many parts of the
kingdom. Beyond all cavil, whatever may
have been the neglect and aversion in a following year, the immediate response of the English court and people to this appeal, was nobly
generous, to such extent that nothing else like
it can be cited from the history of centuries
before our own. No doubt one strong motive
with the authorities was found in the absolute
necessity of the case. They could not have
these Palatines perish by starvation in their
streets. Something must be done to keep life
in them while in London, and something also
to rid London of their burden. But far more
than this, which the closest self-interest would

demand, the appeal seems to have touched the chord of sympathy in the English heart in both city and country. Queen Anne, who, though lacking in many of the qualities needful, not only for a monarch, but also for a strong character, was of tender heart, became greatly interested and took the poor people under her special care. This care aided them effectively at the first, and would have protected them against some of the oppressions of the near future, had she possessed tenacity of purpose and strength of will to resist squabbling politicians.

The immediate needs of the people were met in a way which for that day must be accounted magnificent. The Queen allowed ninepence each per day for present subsistence, and lodgings were provided in various parts of London. One thousand tents, taken from the army stores and pitched on the Surrey side of the Thames, sheltered the greater number. Fourteen hundred were lodged for four months in the warehouses of Sir Charles Cox. Many occupied barns until they were needed for the crops. A smaller number found lodgment in empty dwellings, while the few among them with means obtained quarters at the inns.   In some instances buildings were put up for them, of which a monument still remains in a hamlet at the west of London, where four buildings, yet called "the Palatine Houses," were erected for these people by the Parish of Newington.   Much of this generous provision was due to the kindly interest of the Queen, who not only gave of her own purse, and incited her government to similar action, but issued briefs calling for collections throughout the kingdom.   It is estimated that the sums, expended by the government and contributed by the people of England for the support and final establishment of the Palatines in Ireland and America, aggregated the enormous amount of £135,000.*

Of course, the question of the future disposition of these people was as urgent as their immediate subsistence.   Mortimer says that there was no settled plan (among the Palatines) for their settlement anywhere.   Burnet seems to agree with him, and represents that the people in the Palatinate were "so ravished"

* *Trans. Alb. Ins.*, 1871, p. 107. Burnet, iv., 63. Mortimer, iii., 233.

by the report of what kindness had been
shown to Kockerthal and his companions
in London, that these thousands pressed
thither to throw themselves in like manner
on the bounty of the Queen. The intima-
tions, however, are numerous in the colonial
records that the emigration was with the
intention of reaching America at last. To
be sent thither was the first request of Kockerthal, and the first request also of this larger
body of emigrants. America evidently was
to them the land of promise, where only
their exodus could find its object. True, in
their destitution of all means towards reaching their hope, they had to put themselves
on the generous consideration of the English
government,—and were compelled also to submit themselves to its discretion and direction. Yet a settlement in America was the
constant object of their desire. The long
delay of months in London acted upon some
of them as a discouragement, and they were
quite ready to turn their steps towards other
locations. Not a few of the men enlisted in
the British army, and perhaps a few hundreds,
wandering singly—or in small companies—

through the rural parts of England, found permanent homes in its scattered towns and villages. Some also remained in London, going into domestic service or finding engagements in their special handicrafts. Some were sent by the authorities back to their native country, on account of their religious faith.* It was stated that about one tenth of the emigrants were Roman Catholics, whose presence among their Protestant countrymen can be easily explained by the natural desire for either adventure or improvement of condition. The government would not send men of their faith into the colonies, neither was it willing to permit their prolonged residence in England. In consequence of this disposition and the pressure thereby brought to bear upon these Romanists, many of them became Protestants, while those who were tenacious of their faith were returned under government passports to the Palatinate.

But, though the reduction in numbers by all these means was considerable, the great mass still remained to tax the ingenuity of the authorities. The emphatic recognition of the

* Luttrell's *Diary*, vi., 473, 489.

grave character of the situation is well expressed by the high rank of those who were at first charged with the care of these people. The receipt and distribution of money for their relief, and the duty of considering and suggesting plans for their disposal, were put into the hands of a committee, appointed by the Queen, on which were persons of so exalted station as the Archbishop of Canterbury and the Lord High Chancellor.

The first suggestion was to settle the people in various parts of England as, if feasible, attended by the least expense. By parcelling them out in small companies among the hundreds of the English counties, the entire volume could easily be absorbed into the community, and in time would add to the national wealth. The nature of the Parish Laws, however, was such as to present so many obstacles to the scheme, that it was decided to be impracticable.

It was also proposed to settle them in a body in the New Forest of Hampshire, where * lands could be parcelled out to them by shares or lots from the royal demesnes. This also

* Mortimer's *England*, iii., 233.

proved only a futile suggestion.   To establish
a foreign community in the heart of England
was regarded as dangerous to the welfare
of the nation.   Doubtless also the tenacity
with which the great majority of the Palatines
held to their desire of transportation to
America, went far to discourage all attempts
to make for them an English domicile.   Luttrell * states that the merchants of Bedford
and Barnstaple, who were engaged in the
New Foundland fisheries, designed employing
five hundred of them in their service.   This
may have been done,—and it is altogether probable that in such ways many of the people
were provided for.   Indeed, some disposition
of the kind, the employment on land and sea
in various trades, must have taken place with
regard to a very considerable number.   Otherwise we cannot account for the disparity
between the numbers reported in London in
October of 1709, and the aggregate of the
several recorded shipments of them out of
England.   These amount to the sum of seven
thousand and five hundred persons.   This
aggregate, in case the statement is correct

* *Diary*, vi., 496.

that the number coming into England was thirteen thousand, would leave over five thousand to be otherwise accounted for. But of this there is no record, and their final disposition must be set down to the score of various employments within the kingdom, and unrecorded dispersions into many parts of the country.

There were three large shipments of the people, of which record is made. The first was to Ireland, of which only brief account need be here made. To the Commissioners, pondering over the problem of the proper disposition of the Palatines, the Lord Lieutenant of Ireland represented that land and occupation for a large number of them could be found in his government. The proposition, being approved by the Commissioners and the Queen, was laid before Parliament, which voted £24,000 for the transportation of the company sent thither and their immediate subsistence upon arrival.* Five hundred families, comprising thirty-eight hundred souls were at once sent over. Luttrell writes, under

* Mort. *Eng.*, iii., 233,
Luttrell's *Diary*, vi., 474.
Larned's *Hist. for Ready Reference*, iv., 2412.

date of 9th of August, 1709, "An abundance
of them are gone hence in waggons for Ches-
ter, to embark for Ireland." They were settled in Munster, where, being provided with
land, they soon made for themselves homes
and became a sturdy stock, useful and influential in the country.* The English traveller,
Farrar, writes of them, early in the present
century : " They [their descendants] have left
off sauer-kraut and taken up potatoes, tho
still preserving their own language. . . .
Their superstitions still savor the banks of the
Rhine, and in their dealing they are upright
and honorable." Kohl, a German traveller,
in 1840, writes of them that "they had not
lost their home character for probity and
honor, and are much wealthier than their
neighbors."

The second large shipment of the Palatines
was to the Carolinas. They sailed from England in the early autumn of 1709. The expedition was at the suggestion of two natives of
Berne, one a nobleman named Cristopher de
Graffenried, and the other Lewis Michell, a
merchant. Of the two, De Graffenried was

Penn. Hist. Mag., x., 381.

the controlling spirit in their associated affairs,
and finally, for some reason which does not
appear, seems to have engrossed them all, as
in the subsequent story he alone appears to be
considered as of responsibility and authority.
Michell, at this time a resident in London,
had spent years in America, having been sent
thither by the Canton of Berne to look for a
location for a colony.   The two associates had
bought of the Carolina Proprietaries ten thousand acres of land between the Neuse and
Cape Fear rivers, paying for them twenty
shillings sterling for each one hundred acres,
and at a yearly rental of six pence per one
hundred acres.*   They had also agreed with
the authorities that the Surveyor General
should lay out for them in addition to this
tract one hundred thousand acres more, to be
held for them twelve years, probably with an
option to assume the ownership thereof according as the success or failure of the colonizing
scheme might dictate.   It is noted that the
title to these lands was vested in De Graffenried alone, and because of this great estate,
together with his semi-lordship over the colon-

* Hawks's *N. Carolina*, ii., 86.

ists, he received the title of Landgrave. In many of the colonial references he is called Baron.

Williamson * writes : "This company, having secured the lands, wished to make them productive by settling them with tenants, and the poor Palatines presented themselves as an object of speculation." To this language Hawks makes strenuous exception, as quite careless and also unworthy of the circumstances. Such objection were certainly valid if it were to be considered as reflecting upon the Palatines and the worthiness of their cause. But this reflection is not necessarily involved, and so far as De Graffenried's subsequent conduct can declare his motive at the beginning of the enterprise, the language can hardly be declared unjust as applied to him. It would appear that the two associates, having gotten possession of the land for the projected colony, reported thereon to the cantonal authorities of Berne, by whom Michell had been sent on his prospecting tour. For, when they enter into the story of the Palatines, they are already accompanied in London by a considerable num-

* *History of N. Carolina*, i., 183.

ber of Swiss, who may be supposed to have
been attracted to their enterprise by their report. Possibly some of these Swiss, if not all,
may have been sent by the government of
Berne, in pursuance of the plan which had
suggested sending an agent to America.
However that may be, the beginnings of the
Swiss colony were with De Graffenried and
Michell in London in the summer of 1709, at
the time when the Queen and Council, the
Lords of Trade and the Parliament were trying
to solve the problem of the Palatines. Of
the volume of this Swiss contingent no exact
record is preserved. One account sets it at
fifteen hundred, but this can hardly be considered as correct. Probably their number was less
than half so great ; at all events, sufficiently
small not to dominate the Palatine element in
the new settlement ; for whatever their number,
that settlement was constantly known as Palatine, so spoken of by De Graffenried and by the
Carolina authorities. It is safe to suppose that
the associates looked upon this Swiss emigration as not large enough for the needs and
success of their enterprise. Hence they were
quick to see the advantage presented by the

Palatines seeking a home and the authorities seeking relief from the burden of their support. They soon approached the Commissioners with propositions to take some of this "poor people " to their new plantation in Carolina. Luttrell* records, under date of 6 Oct. 1709, that "the Commissioners about the poor Palatines had resolved to send forthwith 600 to Carolina," Another hundred should be added to this as the number of the Palatines who came to this country with De Graffenried.

The Articles of Agreement between "the Commissioners and Trustees under the Queen's bounty for the subsistence and settlement of the German Palatines," and the two associates, make a very interesting document, as illustrating not only the destitute condition of that people, but the large spirit of generosity and care toward them, which at first possessed the English mind. Some of its expressions and provisions should be here quoted.† It recites the purchase of land by De Graffenried and Michell, " now waste and good for settlement," and says that the Commissioners

---

* *Diary*, vi., 496.
† Hawks's *N. Carolina*, ii., 54.

"thought fit to dispose of, for this purpose, six hundred persons of the said Palatines, which may be ninety-two families more or less—they have laid out and disposed of to each of the said six hundred poor Palatines the sum of twenty shillings in clothes—and likewise paid to said De Graffenried and Michell the sum of five pd. ten sh. for each, for transportation to North Carolina and comfortable support there."

The agents are "within two days to embark them in two ships, for North Carolina, and provide for them on the way." After arrival in the new settlement the agents are "within three months to have surveyed two hundred and fifty acres for each family, to be divided to each by lot, to be contiguous for the sake of society and of religion." This land was to be given to them in fee, to hold free of rent for five years, and afterwards at a rental of two pence per acre.

During the first year the partners were to supply to the "said poor Palatines sufficient quantities of grain and other provisions and necessaries for their comfortable support and relief,"—such outlay to be repaid by the Palatines at the end of three years. Also, "within four months" they were to "provide to each family two cows, two calves, two sows with their last litter, two ewe sheep and two lambs, with a male of each of said kind of cattle to propagate and increase." This is to be repaid by the Palatines at the end of seven years. In addition the partners, "immediately after the partition of the land, shall give and dispose of *gratis* a sufficient quantity of tools for working the ground and building houses." It is also directed that "the conveyances of land shall be registered," and that "beyond what stipulations are herein contained" De Graffenried and Michell, their heirs and assigns, shall have no further claim against the settlers. Then, as making still more positive the benevolent purposes of the Commissioners, it is further enjoined that "these articles are to be construed in the most favorable sense for the ease, comfort, and advantage of the said poor Palatines, and in cases of difficulty the Governor of North Carolina shall decide in conformity with this agreement and contract."

Evidently, thus far in their migration, the poor people had fallen into very kindly hands, and one can hardly imagine more favorable disposition towards a band of destitute emigrants. To the extent that a formal agreement

could effect, the establishment of this colony
was under most auspicious conditions. These,
however, were not all fulfilled.

The voyage across the Atlantic, begun early
in October and completed late in December,
1709, was remarkably quick for that day of
ocean travel. The expedition ascended the
Neuse River to the junction of the Trent, and
there landing began their first settlement, to
which they gave the name of New Berne, in
memory of the native city of the two Swiss'
partners. Here and in the neighboring country, chiefly on the borders of the streams, the
people settled down, cleared portions of the
land and built their humble homes, confident
of present safe harborage at last and hopeful
of a prosperous future. Not all things, however, were consonant with this hope.

The partners—or, more properly speaking,
De Graffenried, for we hear no more of
Michell in the affair—proved unfaithful to
the contract. The particulars are but meagre,
and it may be that the Baron provided for
the immediate necessities of the people, but
it is certain that he never fulfilled the agreement to allot lands to them in fee. The

Minutes of the Council of North Carolina,*
under date of 6th Nov. 1714, contain a
petition from the Palatines, setting forth that
"they were disappointed of their lands," and
praying the Council that each family, "now
greatly impoverished by the Indian War,"
might be allowed to take up four hundred
acres, on two years' payment.   This petition
was favorably received by the Council and the
case represented to the Proprietaries, with
recommendation that the prayer be granted.
We may suppose, with no injustice to De
Graffenried, that he at no time intended to
give titles to the Palatines.   By what way
he procured the sole title to the entire tract
as vested in himself, to the exclusion of his
partner, Michell, does not appear.   But the
fact that it was so, and that Michell soon
disappears from the enterprise, as tho crowded
out of participation, together with the failure
to give the promised titles to the Palatines,
argue ambitious schemes on the part of De
Graffenried, similar to those entertained by
other great landholders in the colonies, to
found a Barony in North Carolina.   To this

* Hawks, ii., 87.

end he would refrain from conveying any of
the land to other possession than his own,
and keep the entire settlement as tenants on
his Manor. However diverse this is from
his own agreements, it does not seem too
severe a judgment on the facts in hand. On
one occasion he called himself the "King of
the Palatines"—perhaps only to be regarded
as a clever ruse to save himself out of the
murderous hands of the Indians. Yet, taken
in connection with the other facts just noted,
the assumption of that title would indicate
a habit of thought more permanent than a
moment of peril.

The peril, which moved him to assume a
royal style, proved the means of his early
separation from the Palatines and America.
It came upon him suddenly, while exploring
the lands up the Neuse River, which the
Indians regarded as their own and not to be
encroached upon by the whites. De Graffenried was accompanied on this expedition
by a negro servant, and by John Lawson,
who had recently been made Surveyor General of North Carolina.* The Indian tribes

* Williamson's *N. Car.*, i., 188,

along the coast had already been decimated
by disease, rum and conflicts with the English, and were able to offer no further opposition to the advance of the settlements. But
the Tuscaroras, who had had little contact
with the whites, still abode in their strength.
Lawson was already familiar to them and
obnoxious. He had not long since surveyed
two larger tracts, which to the Indians seemed
to threaten their own title, and excited their
anger against him. For this reason they laid
in wait and captured Lawson and his companions, when they had gone some distance
up the Neuse. The prisoners were dragged
before the Indian Council and condemned to
death. It was then that De Graffenried saved
his life by claiming a royal rank, assuring the
Indians that he was not English and had
naught to do with the encroachments of the
English, but was the King of the Palatines,
a peaceful folk, who had recently come to the
country. The assumed dignity imposed upon
the Indians, who spared his life. But it was
not a bar to the slaughter of his companions. They killed both Lawson and the
negro, with the usual refinements of Indian

executions, and after five days suffered De Graffenried to depart. He is said during these days to have formed a treaty with the Indians for the protection of the Palatines, who were not disturbed on the occasion of the massacre at Bath. Some of the terms of the treaty bind the contracting parties "to show friendship towards each other." "No land is to be taken up by the Baron without the consent of the Indians." In case of war between the English and the Indians, the Palatines were to remain neutral. In regard to this last provision, I note that a petition of the Palatines, of somewhat later date, alleges that they "were called out to defend the country, by orders from Edenton (*i. e.*, the Governor), while their Trustee was a prisoner among the Indians."

And so the Baron saved himself alive and returned to his city of New Berne. But the experience seems to have completely disgusted him with America and all schemes of colonization. Shortly thereafter he departed for Virginia or Switzerland, never to come back again to his Palatine kingdom. What he did with his land-title is by no means clear. Wil-

7

liamson says that he mortgaged his whole tract
to Thomas Pollock for £800. This is denied
by Hawks. Another and unknown writer,*
says that he *sold* his estate to Pollock for £800,
and moved to Virginia, to the settlement of
Germans established by Governor Spotswood
at Germanna. It is very probable that the
transaction with Pollock was a sale, but the
removal of De Graffenried to Virginia seems
to be predicated only on the presence there,
fifty years after, of a Metcalf De Graffenried,
probably a grandson of the Baron. At all
events, the Swiss leader disappears from the
Palatine affairs.

After his departure, the people, as Williamson writes,

"being industrious and living in a country where
land was plenty and cheap, increased in number and
acquired property. After many years, upon their petition to the king, they were in some measure indem-
nified by a grant of land of ten thousand acres, free
from quit-rents for ten years." †

The treaty of the Baron with the Indians
did not effectually protect the settlement which,
two years afterwards, suffered a loss by massacre of one hundred and twelve.‡ In con-

---

Virginia Historical Coll. New Series, v., 134, 135.
† v., 185.   ‡ Martin's *Hist. of N. Car.*, i., 245.

sequence of this severe experience many of
the people are said to have removed to the
less exposed settlement in Virginia, where
many of their countrymen had already found
a home. But by far the greater number remained to build up the city and country of their
first settlement, where many local marks and
living names bear witness of their foundation.

Of the Palatine settlement in Virginia a few
words should be written, and only a few words
are possible, so indefinite are the notices of it
on public record and in colonial history. The
settlement was a special pet of Governor Spotswood, and was by him "founded on a horse-
shoe peninsula of four hundred acres in the
Rapidan. The little town was called Germanna, after the Germans sent over by Queen
Anne and settled in that quarter." * This was
a " settlement of German Protestants, recently
effected under the Governor's auspices in a region hitherto unpeopled on the Rapidan." †
This is about all that is recorded of the origin
of the settlement at Germanna. But it is not
difficult to supply some items by means of the
argument of probabilities. Gov. Spotswood

* *Virg. Hist. Soc.*, i., pp. x., xiii.
† Campbell's *Hist. of Virginia*, p. 381.

was in London, and was appointed to his government of Virginia, at the time when the Palatines were awaiting in that city the disposition to be made for them by the government. The large companies to Ireland and North Carolina had already been forwarded, and matters were in train for shipping to New York with Governor Hunter some three thousand more. As Spotswood arrived in Virginia in June of 1710, the same month in which Hunter landed at New York, his departure and Hunter's from England must have been at about the same time: and although there is no record accessible of any contract or orders to him to care for a colony of Palatines, it seems to be certain that the Queen and the Commissioners did not fail to avail themselves of the opportunity afforded by his departure to provide for still another portion of that people. How large the company was we have, of course, no means of telling, but they doubtless came over with Spotswood under the commendation and at the expense of the Queen. Spotswood himself was a man of generous nature, felt a sympathy for the suffering and destitute people, took constant interest in them and opened iron mines in the vicinity, both for their employment and his own profit. At the expiration of his official life he did not return to England, but retired to Germanna, among his beloved Palatines, and there built for himself a home of palatial proportions for the day and place, described by Spotswood's friend, Col. William Byrd * as "an enchanted castle." The locality, the fortunes of the first settlers and the character and hospitality of Spotswood, seem to have made this settlement of the Palatines the subject of much tradition, very little of which has gone upon record. Conway says,† "The Germans he [Spotswood] imported had a curious story, yet to be told ; and the town Germanna which he founded on the upper Rappahannock is the haunt of romance."

Some ten or fifteen years after Spotswood's retirement to Germanna, a company of Germans came into Virginia from Pennsylvania, doubtless Palatines from Berks County. They took up forty thousand acres in the lower Shenandoah valley, and founded the town of Strasburg, just over the mountain from Ger-

* Magill's *Hist. of Virginia*, p. 122.
† *Barons of the Potomac*, p. 18.

manna.*   It is not only of this later immigration, but also of its predecessor, that we are to understand Cooke's words : " To this day, the Germans constitute an element of the population, and in some places the language is still spoken."   In a spirit of high commendation of this stock, Prof. Henneman † (whose name would seem to indicate for himself a Palatine extraction) says :

"The German element seems at first sight not to have been so pronounced as might have been expected from their early contact.   This is due in large measure to their natural conservatism and their contentment, clustering by themselves, to lead simple, thrifty, and comparatively secluded lives.   In reality the geography of the State has been deeply affected, as the number of post-offices bearing German appellations testify.   William Wirt, Judges Conrad and Sheffey ‡ and Governors Kemper, Koiner and Speece are among the prominent representatives of this race."

* Cooke's *Hist. of Virginia*, p. 323.
† *Virg. Hist. Coll.* New Series, xi., 30.
‡ Probably a derivative from the name Schoeffer.

CHAPTER IV.

THE EXPERIMENT.

WE return now to London, and the inception of that enterprise, which brought with Governor Hunter to New York nearly three thousand of the Palatines. This is the special immigration of these people, which is best known, and generally supposed to be referred to when any allusion is made to the coming of the Palatines to this country. The story of it is well worth exactness of narrative, by which sundry misunderstandings may be corrected.

While the Palatines were yet in London, and the authorities perplexed as to the best way in which to "dispose of" them, there came to England an important delegation from the Province of New York. The chief per-

sons in it were Peter Schuyler, the Mayor of
Albany, and Col. Nicholson, one of Her Majesty's officers in America. Their mission was
to urge by personal presence and speech, more
urgently than was possible to any written appeal, the need of more generous measures on
the part of the home government for the defence of the province against the French and
their allied Indians. In the recent past the
attacks of these foes had been very persistent
and severe, while the colonists felt that the
government of England had neglected to
afford them all the support and aid which were
their due. Col. Schuyler, by a happy and inventive thought, conceived the idea that the
cause would be greatly furthered by taking to
England some Indian chiefs and exhibiting them
"in their barbaric costume,* knowing that the
movements of nations are often caused by the
veriest trifles." He succeeded in inducing five
Sachems of the Mohawks to go with him, and
speedily found that he had contrived a very
efficient scheme. " The arrival of the Sachems
occasioned great observation throughout the

---

* Dunlap's *Hist. of New York*, i., 269.
See also Parkman, *Half Century of Conflict*, i., 141.

kingdom." * Crowds followed them in the
streets, and small pictures of them were widely
sold. " The court was in mourning for the
Prince of Denmark, and the Indians were
dressed in black underclothes, but a scarlet
ingrain cloth mantle was thrown over all other
garments." The English and the Indians
alike were delighted with the exhibition. The
Guards were reviewed for their entertainment,
and they were taken to see the plays in the
theatres. They were given an audience by the
Queen, to whom they presented belts of wam-
pum, and represented that, not only the English colonists, but also the friendly Indians,
needed a more efficient defence against the
French. " The reduction of Canada," they
urged, " would be of great weight to our free
hunting." It is interesting to note that, so far
as promises would go, the scheme of Schuyler
was very successful, and the " government engaged to send to New York a sufficient arma-
ment for the conquest of Canada," which was
not done at that time.

It is possible that one or two of the five
sachems may have been Mohican.† Hopkins

* Holmes's *Annals*, i., 503.
† *Historical Memoirs Relating to the Housatunnuk Indians.* p. 16.
Ruttenber's *Indian Tribes of Hudson's River*, p. 188.

relates that Mr. Sergeant, missionary to the Indians about Stockbridge, took to New Haven for education two lads, one of whom was named " Etowankaum, who, by the way, is Grandson by his mother to Etowankaum, chief of the River Indians [Mohicans], who was in England in Queen Ann's Reign."

One of the five died on the passage to England. Addison in No. 50 of the *Spectator*, and in No. 171 of the *Tatler*, refers to this embassy. The former reference is worth quoting as stating that Addison himself followed the *four* Indian chiefs about, to observe their manners and their effect upon the populace. He gives the names of two of them; Sa Ga Yean Qua Rash Tow, and " E Tow O Koam, King of the Rivers." The forms of these names would almost suggest that they were invented by Addison, but the likeness of the latter to Etowankaum makes them rather illustrative of the gentle essayist's struggles with an unknown tongue. Doubtless the former also was an honest effort to anglicize a genuine name, tho its proper form does not appear. Addison goes on to give portions of a writing by Sa Ga Yean Qua Rash Tow, left

by him at his lodging-place in London. It
purports to be a comment on the sights of
London and the manners of the people, but is
evidently a pure invention of Addison himself,
using the occasion to indulge his amiable satire
upon the foibles of English life, and as a supposed Indian repartee for the abundant comments on themselves by the curious English
mind.

Now, the connection between this Indian
embassy and the Palatines is found in a cir-
cumstance, of which the government made
small account, but which exercised a great
and determining influence on their fortunes.
It so happened that while these chiefs were in
London they came in contact with the Palatines. "In their walks in the outskirts of London they saw the unenviable condition of the
houseless and homeless Germans ; and one of
them, unsolicited and voluntarily, presented the
Queen a tract of his land in Schoharie, N. Y., for
the use and benefit of the distressed Germans."*

Weiser in his autobiography says, that
"five chiefs of the Mohawk Indians saw and
pitied the wretched condition of the people,

* Rupps's *Berks Co.*, p. 189, quoted from *Hallishe Nachrichten.*

and offered to open to the perishing mass their hunting grounds beyond the sea."

This incident, notable and pathetic, seems at first thought quite improbable. We are not wont to think of the Indian as a pitiful benefactor. And yet, tho no other formal record of it is found, we may safely conclude that the story is substantially true. As will be seen, the English authorities, at the outset of the emigration to New York, had in mind that Schoharie was to be the location of the new settlement. We find also frequent references afterwards by the Palatines themselves to Schoharie as "given to the Queen, for them," and as a land already promised to them by the Queen, to which they should be allowed to depart from their desolate condition on the Hudson. It is difficult to account for the prepossession towards that exquisite valley on the frontier, except on the supposition that this gift by the Indian Sachem was actually made. Certainly, the larger portion of these three thousand emigrants left London with Schoharie as the synonym of their hope, and were not satisfied until they looked on its level meadows and lordly hills.

The Commissioners, having sent off to Ireland that large colony, noted in the last chapter, immediately set themselves to devising means for the disposition of the rest of the people. Two days after the contingent bound for Ireland had left London, the Board of Trade made to the Queen additional * suggestions, to the effect that the remainder of the Palatines, or so many of them as possible, be transported at government's cost to America, and be settled on Hudson's River;—that they should be supported for one year and be supplied with all needed tools, and that the Queen should grant to every one, "without fee or reward, the usual and like number of acres as was granted, or directed to be granted, to every one of the Palatines † lately sent thither, and under like conditions." It is suggested tentatively that the people might find employment, alike advantageous to themselves and the government, in the production of Naval Stores. And then, with a startling buoyancy of imagination, the grave Lords of Trade, premising that the colony of Virginia produces many wild grapes, suggests that such of the Palatines

* *Col. Hist. of N. Y.*, v., 72.   † Kockerthal's first company.

as had been accustomed to viticulture might be sent to that plantation, so that through the wine to be made by them " a new and profitable trade might be introduced to the benefit of this Kingdom." This is but one of several tokens that the authorities, at the beginning of their ventures with the Palatines, had very high anticipations of great returns to be made from the enterprises undertaken. Of this prospective wine trade we hear no more ; but it is not at all improbable, that it occupied place in the plans under which, in the following winter, Spotswood took with him to Virginia the colony which settled at Germanna.

This action of the Board of Trade was taken in August, but a delay of several months occurred before any further steps were made towards the execution of its purpose. Meanwhile the Commissioners were interested in sending out the emigration to North Carolina under De Graffenried and Michell ; and the authorities were exercised about the choice of a new governor for the Province of New York, that office having recently become vacant through the death of Lord Lovelace, after a tenure of only a few months.

Their choice settled upon Col. Robert Hunter, a man eminently fitted for the position,
and, as it proved, without a superior among
all the royal governors in the American provinces. He was born in Scotland, of poor
and humble parentage, and while yet a boy
was apprenticed to an apothecary.* Of an
exceedingly active mind, he must have applied himself to its improvement with considerable diligence, for, while not possessed of
any special external educational advantages,
he gives proof of an intellectual cultivation
far above his station and in after life became the friend of Addison, Steele, Swift, and
the other wits of that day. Of an ambitious nature, disdaining the obscure and plod-
ding trade to which he had been bound, he
ran away and enlisted as a common soldier.
He was possessed of great personal beauty and
fine soldierly bearing, qualities which at once
attracted notice, commending him to the favor
of his superiors and resulting in his speedy
promotion from the ranks to high commission.
They also procured for him the attention and
regard of Lady Hay, widow of Lord Hay, who

* Dunlap's *Hist. of N. Y.*, p. 270. Booth's *Hist. of N. Y.*, p. 286.

was the owner of a large fortune.   The affection
between the two soon ripened into marriage,
the beginning of a wedded life of rare devotion
and happiness, and the termination of which,
by the death of Lady Hunter in 1716, made
for the Governor an incurable wound.   In 1707
he was appointed Lt. Governor of Virginia,
and at once sailed for the colony.   His ship,
however, was captured by a French privateer
and taken to France, in which country Hunter
was detained prisoner for several months.   He
was exchanged for the Bishop of Quebec, and
returned to London about the time of the
Palatine sojourn in that city, and was appointed
to succeed Lovelace in the government of New
York.   It is said that he owed this appointment to his friend Addison, at that time Under
Secretary of State, which may be in a measure
true.   If so, we may take it as a proof that
favoritism can at times make the most judicious
choice, for there is small doubt that the honor
and duty of the position could have found no
worthier or better-fitted shoulders on which to
rest.   Nor can there be much doubt that, had
Gov. Hunter been properly supported by the
home government, and had its pledges to him

been fulfilled, his administration of the Province
would have been singularly notable for success.

With the Governor's office the rank of Briga-
dier General was also conferred upon Hunter,
who at once set himself to consider and consult about the affairs of his new government,
prominent among which was the disposition of
the Palatines. For it was evidently settled in
the mind of the Lords of Trade that New York
must be the destination of a large number of
that people, and one may easily suppose that
this thought had large place in the selection
of Hunter for the government of that Province,
on the ground of his well-known capacity.
As the result of his study upon the question,
he made a proposition to the Lords of Trade,
under date of 30 Nov. 1709,* that three thousand of the Palatines be sent with him to New
York, to be employed there in the production·
of Naval Stores ; but he does not suggest in
this note any particular location in the Province.
Some special details are entered into, as that
four persons should be sent out to instruct
the people in the proposed manufacture, and
that he should have leave to employ such clerks

* *Col. Hist.*, v., 112.

and other agents as should be needed ; and
that utensils, tents, fire-locks, hemp-seed, and
other necessaries should be provided. On the
next day he addressed another letter to the
Board suggesting that it was well to

"consider whether it be advisable that they [the Pala-
tines] be *servants* to the Crown for a certain term, or at
least 'till they have repaid the expense the Crown is at
in settling them at work and subsisting them whilst they
cannot subsist themselves ; and afterwards the lands they
possess be granted them in fee, with the reservation of
a reasonable Quit-Rent to the Crown."

These suggestions of Hunter bear fruit in
a few days in a report by the Board of Trade
to the Queen. In this they note that New
York is the "most advanced frontier," as
against the French and hostile Indians, and
that the Palatines, if properly located, might
add greatly to the defence of the province.
As to the place of their settlement, the Board
proposes the region of "the Mohaques and
Hudson's Rivers, where are great numbers
of Pines fit for the production of Turpentine
and Tarr, out of which Rozin and Pitch are
made." They specially indicate "a Tract of
land lying on Mohaques River, fifty miles by

four, and a Tract lying upon a Creek [undoubt-
edly the Schoharie] which runs into said River,
between twenty-four and thirty miles in length,
of which your Majesty has possession." This
possession by the Queen is not here attributed
to the gift of the Indian chief, but to "the
vacating of several extravagant grants." * But
it may not be contended that such description
disproves the story of a gift, which had so
taken possession of the Palatine mind. On
the contrary, it might be argued that the
Indian offer furnished the reason for select-
ing that locality.

The report goes on to advise that the Governor be "empowered to settle them on these
or other lands, in a Boddy, or in separate
settlements, as most fit." Each family should
receive forty acres, "after they shall have·
repaid the government." They should be
prohibited from engaging in "the manufacture of Woollen." After their houses are built

---

* This vacating was enacted in 1698 by the provincial legislature
and was afterwards approved by the Queen. It voided several
enormous patents given by Col. Fletcher, while he was Governor of
New York. Among these was one to a certain Col. Nicholas
Bayard, which conveyed the entire valley of Schoharie. We shall
meet this Bayard again in connection with the Palatine fortunes.

and the ground cleared, they should "be employed in the making of Turpentine, Rozin, Tarr, and Pitch." And the premium to encourage the importation of Naval Stores should be given" to the Factor or Agent, to and for the sole Benefit of such Palatines, who were, the Manufacturers of such stores." * Finally they should be naturalized and "made denizens of this Kingdom." This report with its advice was approved by the Queen, and steps were at once taken to put the scheme into execution.

In the arrangements made, a new element appears, not found or suggested in the previous shipments of the Palatines from London. With the colonies sent to Ireland, North Carolina, and Virginia the government made no contract for service. The people were simply recipients. There was, indeed, a contract in regard to the North Carolina colony, but the parties in contract with the government were the Swiss partners, who were bound to great care and kindness in their treatment of the emigrants. With regard to the colony

* This premium was, some years before, offered by the government to incite the colonists to such manufacture.

to go out with Hunter the course of government was different. The first measure towards setting his scheme on foot was the making of a contract, not with Hunter or the provincial authorities, but with the Palatines themselves. It is plain from that agreement that the government had an eye, no longer solely to the benefit of these people, but to its own profit and advantage. Nor could such purpose be condemned, the hardships to the Palatines proceeding not from the then intention of the government, but from its subsequent failure to fulfil its own part of the contract; and also from the fact that the whole transaction was foredoomed to failure, because involving the presumption that Naval Stores could be produced in places where the natural conditions forbade. By this contract the Palatines bound themselves to become, as Hunter suggested, "Servants to the Crown." The government was to transport them to America and subsist them there; they were to "settle in such place as should be allotted to them"; were to engage in making Naval Stores, all of which they should suffer to be put into her Majesty's storehouses; they were not to attempt the making of any woollen goods ; nor to quit the settlement without the permission of the govenor. After they had by their labor repaid the government for the expenses undertaken for them, they should receive £5 and forty acres of land for each family.*

We may fitly note in this place that the production of Naval Stores in some portion of the Queen's dominions was looked upon by the government as among the most desirable and necessitous of things. Already had England made great advance towards the complete mastery of the sea, fulfilling more and more, in almost each succeeding reign, the promise of Frobisher and Drake. Her merchant ships traversed all ocean paths, and her floating fortresses declared her powers in the most distant seas. To her Admiralty it was a constant burden, that for so many of the materials essential to the making of ships, England had to depend on other nations. Her tar and pitch, and many of her masts and spars, she was forced to buy from Norway, Sweden, and Russia ; while most of the hemp for her cord-

* *Col. Hist.*, v., 117–121.
Doc. Hist., iii., 382 *et seq.*

age was grown on continental fields. The
expense was a heavy tax upon her exchequer,
and the necessity of buying in a foreign mar-
ket was as heavy a burden to her pride.
Hence, as her new empire in America came
to be explored and to disclose something of
its vast resources, one of the chief objects of
search, and a most frequent subject of remark,
was the promise of Naval Stores from the forests of the New World. On this the attention
of the Lords of Trade and the government is
frequently engaged, and diligence to further
this "most noble and laudable work" is urged
upon the colonial authorities with much and
frequent emphasis. In the despatches the
words, Naval Stores, are usually dignified with
capital initials, expressive of the important
nature of the subject.

Many years before the period of the Palatine Immigration the Board of Trade and Colonial governors corresponded in regard to it.
Lord Bellomont, in 1699 (*Col. Hist.*, iv., 501),
writes in lengthened discussion of the feasi-
bility of producing tar and pitch in his Province
of New York. He is enthusiastic over the
certainty of inexhaustible quantities of tar in

the New York forests, and of success in the enterprise, if it is attempted in the right way. He goes into detailed calculations as to methods, cost, and amount of expected returns, and advises the employment of soldiers in the manufacture.

The instructions to Lord Lovelace *—20 July, 1708—urge upon him

" to prevent any impediment to this good work, and to take care that in all new patents for land there be inserted a clause restraining the grantees from Burning the Woods to clear the land, under Penalty of forfeiting their Patent. Likewise a clause making a Particular Reservation to us, Our Heirs and Successors, of all Trees of the diameter of 24 inches and upward, at 12 inches from the ground, for Masts for Our Royal Navy, as also of such other Trees as may be fit to make planks, Knees, etc., for the use of our said Navy."

At a later date Lovelace is directed to use his influence with the colonists towards inducing them to undertake the manufacture of tar and pitch, and other naval stores ; and to offer a premium to all persons who shall send such stores to England.

With the desire for such returns from the colonies thus strong in the governmental mind,

* *Col. Hist.*, v., 55.

we can understand the ardor with which the
Lords of Trade seized upon the proposition of
Gov. Hunter.   For some reason the colonists
had not been moved to the manufacture of the
desired stores, nor had the offered premium
been able to attract them from their fisheries
and farms.   But now the whole matter lies in
the hand of the government.   Here in London
is this great company of Palatines, seeking
asylum and occupation.   There in the colonies
were vast forests of pine, whose shapely stems
and resinous gums waited only for the wood-
man's axe and the tar-bucket.   On the banks
of Hudson's and Mohaques rivers were millions of noble trees, any one of which was fit

> " To be the mast
> Of some great ammiral."

How fortunate the conjunction of circumstances, which, while the great pines of America
waited to be felled, brought to England these
fugitives crying for support ! How fine the
opportunity by which the Admiralty can at
last realize its long-cherished, but hitherto disappointed, dream ! The workers must be
brought to the work. It is interesting and

amusing to note the ardor and enthusiasm with which the authorities adopted the scheme of Hunter, and with what glowing anticipations of assured success they discounted the future. In the Report, in which the Board commends Hunter's proposition to the Queen, they

"take leave to observe that one man may make by his own labor 6 tunns of these Stores in a year, and we have been informed that a number of men, assisting each other, may in proportion make double that quantity, so that, supposing 600 men to be employed in this work, they may produce 7000 tunns of these goods a year : and, if in time a greater quantity of these Stores should be made there than shall be consumed in your Majesty's Dominions, we hope the overplus may turn to a very beneficial trade with Spain and Portugal."

There seems to have been no doubt in the mind of the Lords of Trade that the pines of the Hudson and the Mohawk would furnish all the tar and pitch that England could forever need. The thought was shared by the officials in this country. Thus Hunter, a year afterwards, writes from New York,*—" This great and useful design of providing England forever hereafter with Naval Stores cannot fail other ways than by being let fall at home.—

* *Col. Hist.*, v., 171.

Here is enough for all England forever."
And Du Pré, the Commissary, writes,*

"I am confident that it cannot fail of good success, and
nothing else than the want of support at home can prevent it. There are Tar and pitch enough for supplying,
not only the Royal, but even the whole, Navy of England: and it will give such a life to the Trade of this
Country as may very much contribute to encourage the
Woollen Manufactory at Home, and discourage of it in
the Plantations, by making the returns from this so far
exceed the import, that it will make this Port [New
York] the emporium of the Continent of America."

There is, indeed, no doubt that New York
has become such emporium; but despite the
efforts and prophecies of the Lords of Trade
and their subordinates, its achievement of
that position cannot be set down to the production of Naval Stores. One other glowing prediction is worthy of place here. It is
from the pen of John Bridger, the Instructor
of the Palatines in tar-making, who writes to
the Board of Trade,† "There is enough for
all Britain and this Government [New York],
with the others on this Continent—and it will
be capable of making Great Britain the mart
of all Europe for Naval Stores."

* *Col. Hist.*, v., 172. *Doc. Hist.*, iii., 390. † *Col. Hist.*, v., 174.

Hence the instructions of the Queen to Hunter, on the eve of starting for New York, lay great stress upon this scheme, which at the time of his setting forth was regarded by the Home government as the most important duty of his commission, and which, for several years after the London authorities had ceased to interest themselves in it, still retained its hold upon the opinion and desire of the Governor. The royal orders recite,*

"We being informed that our Province of New York do's abound with vast numbers of Pine Trees proper for the production of Pitch and Tar—[and] Masts for our First-rate ships of War, and Oaks and other Trees fit for beams, knees, planks, and other uses of our Navy Royal —you are to apply your utmost care and diligence towards the promoting of so necessary a Work."

There is an uncertainty as to the precise date of Hunter's departure from England with the Palatines. Luttrell, on 29 Dec., 1709, writes, "Collonel Hunter designs, next week to embark for his government at New York, and most of the Palatines remaining here goe with him to people that colony." Weiser's reminiscences relate, "About Christmas-day

* *Col. Hist.*, v., 141.

(1709) we embarked, and ten ship loads with
about four thousand souls were sent to America." As Weiser was but a boy of twelve at
the time, there might easily have been some
confusion, as to the exact date, in his later
years, as there was in regard to numbers.
The royal instructions to the new Governor
bear date of 20th January, 1710, and presumably were committed to him in London.

Towards the end of January, then, we
may suppose this largest of immigrations to
America in the colonial era to have left the
shores of England. The people were in ten
ships, which made an unusual and imposing
fleet. The number of the Palatines embarked
must be set much below the figures given by
Weiser. In reality there were about three
thousand of them. Discrepancies exist in the
various statements upon this point, and no
official record of the number actually embarked
has been preserved. But their number was
large enough to crowd the small ships of that
day almost to suffocation, and, pitiful as the
tale is, it brings no surprise to learn that nearly
one sixth of the whole number perished by the
way. The voyage was longer than usual by

reason of heavy storms and contrary winds.
From near the end of January until after the
beginning of June, and for some until into
July, the weary people were battling their slow
way across the Atlantic. The crowded quarters, the foul air and insufficient food, made
them the easy prey of disease, so that every day
witnessed the consignment of their dead into
the sea. The mortality was terrible and must
have covered the fleet as with the shadow of
death. Hunter writes from New York on
16th June, 1710, "I arrived here two days
ago. We want still three of the Palatine
ships, and those arrived are in deplorable
sickly condition."

The ships were separated by the weather,
and the first to arrive at New York, anticipating the vessel which carried the Governor, was
the ship *Lyon*, loaded with Palatines. The
authorities of the town were alarmed by the
unhealthful condition of the emigrants, among
whom, it was reported, were "many contagious
diseases" (cases). It was decided to keep
them out of the city and to land them on Nutten (now Governor's) Island, and to build huts
for them. The full tale of the ships was not

made out until near the end of July, when
Hunter writes that

"All the Palatine ships, separated by the weather, are
since arrived, except the *Herbert* Frigate. She was cast
away on the East end of Long Island, on the 7th July.
The men are safe, but our goods are much damaged.
The poor people are mighty sickly, but recover apace.
We have lost above 470 of our number." *

This loss of the *Herbert* is undoubtedly the
historical incident, which gave rise to the legend
of the Palatine Ship and Light.   The legend
is localized on Block, or Manisees, Island,
rather than Long Island, but such transfer-
rence is easy to legendary lore : and, indeed, it
is not impossible that, despite the Governor's
statement, the ship may have gone ashore on
the former island.   The legend by a curious
heterophemy gives the name of the people to
the ship, which becomes in the story, not the
frigate *Herbert*, but the ship *Palatine*, supposed
to be a merchantman laden with goodly cargo.
The tradition represents that the vessel was
decoyed ashore by false beacons, and then
rifled and burned by the islanders, who steadied
themselves for their crime by saying to each

* *Col. Hist.*, v., 166.

other that "dead men tell no tales." But the spirits of the lost ship and crew do not suffer the wreckers to rest without a frequent reminder of their villainy.*

"A light is at times seen from the island upon the surface of the ocean, which in its form has suggested to the imagination a resemblance to a burning ship under full sail; and it is called the Palatine Light and Palatine Ship."

Hunter says that "the men were saved." He may have meant by this the English sailors, while some of the Palatines were lost. This is suggested by the fact that to this day are shown on the west shore of Block Island some almost obliterated graves, said to be of lost seamen of the ship *Palatine*.

Whittier has set the legend in his exquisite poem, "The Palatine," in which he also gives the name of the people to their ship:

"Into the teeth of death she sped :
(May God forgive the hands that fed
The false lights over the rocky Head !)

. . . .

But the year went round, and when once more,
Along their foam-white curves of shore,
They heard the line storm rave and roar,

Penn. Mag. of Hist., xi., 243.

Behold ! again with shimmer and shine,
Over the rocks and the seething brine,
The flaming wreck of the Palatine !

   .   .   .   .   .

For still, on many a moonless night,
From Kingston Head and from Montauk light,
The spectre kindles and burns in sight.

Now low and dim, now clear and higher,
Leaps up the terrible Ghost of Fire,
Then, slowly sinking, the flames expire.

And the wise Sound skippers, though skies be fine,
Reef their sails when they see the sign
Of the blazing wreck of the Palatine ! "

As the several ships of the fleet came into
port, the Palatines were all landed upon Nutten Island, at first for the purposes of quaran-
tine, and afterwards for convenience sake.
Their numbers were quite sufficient for a community by themselves, and altogether too large
for the little city of New York to care for in
its homes and inns. Proclamation was made
to prevent extortion in the price of bread and
other provisions. The Attorney-General was
instructed to devise a plan for the government
of the Palatines, and commissions as Justices of
the Peace were issued to some of their own

number "to hear small causes," such as might arise among themselves.

The chief one of these Justices, and the most prominent and influential man in the entire company, was John Conrad Weiser. He was the father of the Conrad Weiser to whom reference has been made, and was himself the son of a magistrate of Great Anspach, a town in the Duchy of Wurtemburg. He was educated, followed for a while the vocation of a baker, and in his turn rose to the magistracy of the town. He married Anna Magdalena Uebele, whose character was such as to impress her son Conrad with a profound and life-long reverence. She died in 1709, while giving birth to her sixteenth child. Her death was the crowning affliction for her husband. Personal and domestic sorrow was added to national calamities, and by stress of it he was led to join the emigrating thousands, bringing with him all of his children save two daughters, who had married.

It is possible, as noted in the last chapter, that Kockerthal was with this large company. If so, Weiser shared in his counsels and exercised an equal influence upon the people. It is probable also that, on arrival at New York, Kockerthal went to his parish and glebe at Quassaick, leaving Weiser easily the chief among his people. Many complaints were afterwards made about Weiser by the authorities and others interested in oppressing the Palatines. He is called, "rascal," "villain," "riotous," "ringleader of all mischief"; and at one time a warrant was issued for his arrest on a charge of sedition. But the truth was, that those actions, which earned such epithets and attention, were due to the oppressions under which the Palatines were made to suffer. Weiser's bold, free spirit refused to submit to the semi-slavery in which the authorities proposed to hold the people, and he chose such means of resistance as lay ready to his hand. He was seditious only as every revolutionary patriot was seditious.

The sojourn of the people on Nutten Island continued through five months, while the Governor was examining and prospecting after the most promising spot for their permanent establishment. There is an added proof, that the tale of the Indian gift of Schoharie was at least partially true, in the fact that [*] Hunter, very soon after arrival, despatched the Surveyor-General of the province "to survey the land on the Mohaques River, particularly the Skohare, to which the Indians have no pretence." Certainly, it is significant that this should have been the first spot looked at ; and no great pressure is needed upon the words, "have no pretence," to see in them a recognition of the fact, that the Indians by their gift had surrendered all title to those lands.

While waiting the return and report of the Surveyor, the Governor issued an order for apprenticing children of the Palatines, which may be set down as the first of the oppressive actions of the government towards those people.   Hitherto, it would seem that all the measures of the authorities in regard to them had been under the law of kindness.   Beyond question the treatment dealt to them in England was munificent, and no objection could lie against the contract of service, supposing it to be faithfully and fairly executed.   Nor could the sufferings and mortality of the voyage be chargeable to the authorities.

[*] *Col. Hist.*, v., 167.

They were more truly due to the stormy seas which protracted the voyage to nearly double the usual length of time. But there was something in this apprenticing of the children which the Palatines seemed to have regarded as peculiarly oppressive. In their statement of grievances, made some years later, they recite with much pathos, "He took away our children from us without and against our consent." But the probabilities are that the Governor was helpless in the matter. Many of the children were orphans, one or both of the parents having died upon the ocean. These the authorities could not keep dependent on public support, nor could their poor fellow-countrymen provide for them. The only thing possible was to put them to service or trades, and thus in homes, where they would be cared for and would learn to support themselves. It is possible that some of the children were taken from parents unwilling to let them go, but of this we have no proof beyond the statement just quoted, the force of which is qualified by the presumption that, in the complaint against the government every available argument and item would be used.

Not improbably the action of the Governor
was with an arbitrary and imperious manner,
but it does not appear that anything else could
have been done under the circumstances.*
There is preserved in the colonial documents
a list of some of these apprenticed children,
possibly all of them, eighty-four in number,
giving their names and ages, and the names
and residences of their masters. In the list
some things may be noted with interest, as
that two sons, George and Frederick, of John
Conrad Weiser were among those bound out.
Also that Robert Livingston of the Manor
had indentured to him no less than seven of
the children. We observe also that the places
of residence of the masters are widely scattered, from Albany to Long Island, from
Rhode Island to New Jersey. These distances, of course, meant at that time much
more of separation than they would to-day.
With many of these children the distance
effected life-long separation from, and ignorance of, their kindred. Conrad Weiser said
in later years that, when his brothers were
apprenticed, they were lost to the family

*Doc. Hist., iii., 341. See Note II.

forever, and he knew not what had become of them.

But the chief note of interest in this list is found in a certain lad, thirteen years of age, John Peter Zenger by name, whose father had died at sea, and who was apprenticed to one William Bradford, a printer of New York. The name of this lad it behoves every lover of American liberty to remember, and no apology is needed to arrest the current of our immediate story in order to tell in few words what he did for the country of his adoption.*

After Zenger had grown to manhood, there arose a fierce quarrel between Governor Cosby and the Council on the question of salary, which was ever a mooted question between the Royal Governors and the Provincial legislature in New York, and often employed by the latter for the malicious harassment of the Governor. On this occasion the quarrel waxed so strong that the Governor carried it into the court for a mandamus requiring the concession of his claim. The court, supposed to be biassed by reason of the fact that the Chief-Justice, De Lancey, and Justice Philipse sat

* Booth's *Hist. of New York*, p. 329 *et seq.*

upon the bench by the Governor's appointment and at his pleasure, decided against the Council, and issued the mandamus. At this decision the whole city was roused, and the popular indignation found voice at the hand of Zenger. His former employer, Bradford, published the *New York Gazette*, which espoused the Governor's cause; and in opposition thereto, Zenger, who had gone into business as a printer for himself, and was also the Collector of Taxes, started a newspaper, the *New York Weekly Journal*, which was first issued on the 5th of Nov. 1733, and at once assailed the Governor. It abounded in "caustic articles satirizing the Court. All colonial grievances were taken up and fearlessly discussed." The authorship of the articles was attributed to William Smith and James Alexander, advocates, who through government influence had been defeated as candidates for the Council. The government was highly incensed by the *Journal*, and ordered four numbers of it to be publicly burned by the hangman, in the presence of the Mayor and city magistrates. But the city courts refused to receive the order and forbade its execution by the hangman;

and the only way in which the order was
carried out was by a negro slave of the Sheriff,
in the absence of the magistrates.   This could
not satisfy the government, which promptly
arrested Zenger and threw him into prison,
denying to him pen, ink, and paper.   Being
brought up on *habeas corpus*, the court demanded so excessive bail, that he had to return to prison, where he continued to edit his
paper, whispering his instructions to his em-
ployees through the chinks in the door.   The
Grand Jury refused to indict him, but the
Attorney-General filed an Information for
Seditious Libel against him, and he was ar-
raigned for trial by the court he had satirized.
His council were Smith and Alexander, who
began by excepting to the commissions of
the Chief-Justice and Justice Philipse, because
they ran "during pleasure."   This objection
so enraged the court that the advocates were
at once disbarred, and the case adjourned.
There was no other advocate in the city who
dared to appear for Zenger, whose friends sent
to Philadelphia, and secured the services of
the celebrated Andrew Hamilton, long at the
head of the Pennsylvania bar and without a

superior in all the colonies. At this time he
was eighty years old, but still in full vigor of
both mind and body. Without impugning in
any way the character or integrity of the Court,
Hamilton's plea was a triumphant defence of
his client and "the first vindication of the liberty of the Press in America." "The verdict
of acquittal will stand as the first trumpet of
American Independence."

The main items of the story—the attack of
the government on the press and the triumphant vindication of its rights and liberty by
the great lawyer and patriot—are well known
to most Americans. Not so many know that
the first blows in the struggle—so pregnant for
the future of American freedom and citizen-
ship—were struck by the hand of a Palatine.
The story of his countrymen, coming hither
in their poverty and distress, has been often
slighted and disesteemed, and yet it cannot be
properly told without the tale of Zenger's bold-
ness, tenacity and love of right, wherefrom
thus early came into American institutions one
of their greatest blessings and bulwarks. To
get established that for which he fought were
worth all the expense, suffering, and labor of

the Immigration. It may be said, indeed, that
Zenger himself can hardly be credited with any
deep consciousness as to the principle involved,
or with any far-reaching plan to define and con-
serve the rights of humanity. This doubtless
is true; but the same is true also of the vast
majority of men who have risen against wrong
and oppression, and by their work have laid
the generations under tribute. They have
simply known where the yoke galled them, and
have striven to throw it off. Few leaders of
men are like Sam. Adams, who was almost
unique in his foresight of the end from the beginning. To most it falls only to give occasion by their resolute fearlessness for the advent
of a blessing, of the full form of which they
have small conception. So it is that to have
given occasion for the establishment of a Free
Press is an imperishable honor to be set down
to the credit of Zenger, and to be noted as
among the benefits ministered to America by
the children of the Palatines.

We return again to the company on Nutten
Island, whose settlement in a permanent home
was giving the Governor no little trouble. The
report of the Surveyor, or the attractiveness

of some other place, dislodged from his mind
the idea of placing them at Schoharie. He
writes, " It is no wise fit for the design in hand.
There is good lands, but no pine." At a later
period he admits that pine may be found in
that region. Du Pré, who went to London in
the Governor's interest, alleged that the Mohawk had a " fall of six hundred feet," so that
the transportation of the tar and pitch to tide-
water would be very difficult. By this " fall,"
of course, he did not mean a cataract, but the
descent of the stream from the confluence of
the Schoharie to the Hudson. The exaggeration may have been made in ignorance and
from guess-work. The actual descent is not
much above two hundred feet. After the failure on the Hudson, and the departure of many
of the people to the Schoharie—both to be yet
narrated—the Governor suggests that those
who had gone thither " might be employed in
the vast pine forests near Albany."

It is probable that the great distance of Schoharie from New York had about as much influence as any other consideration on his mind.
He is confident that he " will be able to carry
it on elsewhere. There is no want of Pine, but

the Pine land being good for nothing, the difficulty will ly in finding such a situation as will afford good land for their settlements near the Pine lands." Then he says, " I am in terms with some who have lands on Hudson's River fitt for that purpose." Presently, on October 3d, he reports a purchase of land, and on November 14th writes, " I have just returned from settling the Palatines on Hudson's River," and describes the location as a tract of six thousand acres which he had bought from Robert Livingston, for " 400 pds. this country money — £266 English, adjacent to the Pines." Also, as this tract was not large enough for settling and employing all the people, he had placed some of them on a tract " over against it," on the west side of the river, " near Sawyer's Creek," on lands " a mile in length " and having about eight hundred acres, " belonging to the Queen." The Governor writes of the two settlements :

" Each family hath a sufficient lot of good arrable land, and ships of fifteen foot draught of Water can sail up as far as their Plantations. They have already built themselves comfortable huts and are now imployed in clearing the ground. In the Spring I shall set them to work in preparing the trees."

Here again he gives voice to his confidence in
this unfailing source of naval stores.

"I myself have seen Pitch Pine enough upon
the river to serve all Europe with Tarr."

The people were settled by the Governor
in five villages, three of them on the east side
of the river. The number of villages was
shortly increased to seven, and their names
appear as Hunterstown, Queensbury, Annsbury, and Haysbury, on the east side, while
Elizabeth Town, Georgetown, and New Village were situated on the opposite side of
the river. Of these names not one remains.
They had vogue but for a very few years.
Germantown embraced afterwards all the villages on the east side of the river, while those
upon the west were all lost in the town of
Saugerties. The two names of locality in use
among the Palatines, which have survived
until now, are East Camp and West Camp,
though the former only lives in local speech.
West Camp is still a distinct village, and appears on every good map of Ulster County.
In addition to these names, very soon after
the settlement at West Camp, another name,
still surviving, though not appearing in the

official records, Kaatsbaan, was affixed to a locality about two miles to the westward. The old stone church, built there on a rocky knoll in 1732, has bequeathed to its successor of the present day its rear wall, a yet standing witness to the settlement and piety of the Palatines. Besides this, another name, Rhinebeck, on the east side of the river, owes its origin to Palatines who, after the explosion at East Camp, looked a little southward for their homes. This the name of the town implies, while in families still surviving in the town names appearing on the lists of the immigration are represented to this day.

The settlements on the east side were within the domain of the famous Manor of Livingston, which, by various acquisitions at sundry times, by purchase from the Indians, and by royal grants, had become baronial in its proportions. It measured sixteen miles on the river-bank, and stretched eastward twenty-four miles to the Massachusetts line, including the territory now forming the seven townships of Livingston, Copake, Taghkanic, Ancram, Gallatin, Clermont, and Germantown. The first patent covering the most of this domain

was issued to Livingston in 1686 by Governor
Dongan, and in 1714 Hunter gave him a new
patent, erecting the demesne into " one Lord-
ship or Manor," and investing Livingston with
baronial rights, " with power and authority to
establish one Court Leete and one Court
Baron," to try causes arising on the Manor
and to impose fines and penalties.* Hunter's
six thousand acres were mostly within the
limits of the present Germantown—the name
evidently a memorial of this first settlement—
between the river and Roelof Jansen's Kill,
a stream running northwesterly and emptying
into the Hudson near the Manor-House.
Here were settled about two thirds of the
Palatines.

It should be noted that, according to a list
preserved on record, 339 of the refugees
were domiciled in the city of New York.
There were about one hundred more. The
most of them were widows, single women,
and children, unfit for the " great and good
design" of making tar and pitch. In a few
years they were able to build a Lutheran
church. The structure was near Trinity

* *Doc. Hist.*, iii., 416.

Church, and was destroyed by the great fire of 1776. On its site was afterwards erected the first building of Grace Parish.* This New York company seems to have suffered great mortality in the first year, as in September of 1711 a petition from an undertaker in the city, praying payment for two hundred and fifty coffins supplied to the Palatines, is presented to the Governor. Part of these must have been furnished while the great body of the immigrants was on Nutten Island. In any event, this item, together with the account of loss during the voyage, makes a somewhat terrible record. Within eighteen months fully one quarter of the entire number had died.

It should be further noted that in the after experience of trouble and disaster, which came to the settlers up the Hudson, those on the Manor were almost solely involved. It does not appear that any serious effort was made towards the manufacture of naval stores on the west side of the river. Save when the summons was issued for volunteers to serve in the campaign of 1711 against Canada, the more fortunate settlers on this side were, for

* Dunlap's *New York*, p. 270.

10

the most part, left free to build their homes
and turn the forest into farms. Here they
subdued the wilderness and founded families,
many of which live to-day on the ancestral
acres, a sturdy, diligent, thrifty, and God-fear-
ing community.

It is on the East Camp that our attention
must be fixed, and on the effort to turn the
forests of the Hudson into the navy of England. It was a great experiment, well worthy
of attempt under right conditions. Its success
would beyond doubt have ministered im-
mensely to the advantage of the government.
But it was fore-doomed to disastrous failure.
By a very strange obliquity, the scheme, which
had for so many years engaged the attention
of the Home government and the Lords of
Trade, which had enlisted the enthusiasm and
diligence of Governor after Governor, which
had provided so engrossing a topic for correspondence and calculation, and for its initiation
had cost the government so large an outlay of
money, was no sooner set on foot than the
London authorities lost all interest in it and,
without waiting for any demonstration of success or failure, refused to have anything more

to do with the undertaking.   Hunter seems to
have been the only one, whose continuance of
regard for the attempt bore any proper relation
to the zeal of its beginning.   As we shall see,
to him it brought increasing annoyance and
embarrassment, a ruined fortune and reputation and a broken heart; while to the poor
Palatines it occasioned severe suffering, cruel
oppression, mutiny, and flight.

CHAPTER V.

THE FAILURE.

THE three villages in the East Camp contained about twelve hundred people ;
men, women, and children, among
whom the number of able-bodied men must
have been not large. They constituted a
small force with which to carry on " the good
and useful design," supposing that success
therein was among the possibilities. As the
result proved, there were quite enough of them
to demonstrate the futility of the attempt.
The work could not begin at once. The season of their establishment on the Manor was
well advanced into the late fall, no work on
the trees was possible at that time of year, and
the first labors of the people had to be directed
towards housing themselves for the winter.
During that winter, if we are to receive the

THE
PALATINE
SETTLEMENTS
OF THE
HUDSON, MOHAWK
AND SCHOHARIE

statements of the Palatines themselves, they
suffered greatly from the severity of the cold
and the insufficient supply of clothing from the
government. They complained also bitterly
that the supply of food furnished to them was
short of their need and of poor quality.
These statements should, perhaps, be taken
with some grains of allowance, as the unfamil-
iar surroundings and the immediate prospect of
unrequited and compulsory toil may have very
soon moved the people to discontent. In
their extemporized huts, shivering with the
unwonted cold, they had leisure to contrast
their situation and outlook with the good their
fancy had painted, and in pursuit of which they
had come hopefully over the sea, bearing without murmur the sufferings and sorrows of the
voyage. They dwelt in thought on the lands
of the Schoharie, which, they said, " the Queen
had given them " ; and considered that any
action was oppressive which hindered entrance
into that possession. They looked upon their
detention on the Manor as a virtual bondage,
and their obligation to work under the orders
of the authorities as little short of slavery.
This feeling was undoubtedly intensified by the

treatment received from the Governor's agents, who carried themselves as masters among serfs, an attitude and disposition not easily tolerable by men who had resisted oppression and tyranny in the Old World, and for the sake of freedom had come to the new. The discontent found early expression. The snows had hardly disappeared and the people been able to begin the work upon the trees, when Mr. Cast, one of the commissioners over the Palatines, wrote to Governor Hunter, March 1711 :

" The people contemplate their present settlement for a couple of years. I asked Mr. Kockerthal how his people behave. He tells me all are at work and busy, but manifestly with repugnance and merely temporarily ; that the tract intended for them is in their mind a land of Canaan. It is a dangerous time to settle (in Schoharie), and they are willing to have patience for two years. But they will not hear of tar-making."

Mr. Cast's next letter, a few days later, suggests that he had had some trouble with the people, by telling of a better mind in them at that writing. * He writes to Hunter, who seems to have made a visit to allay the trouble, that the people were behaving

* *Col. Hist.*, v., 212.

"as well as could be desired. Those of Queensbury, previously the most perverse, came to tell me they would take the remainder of their share of the Salt-Beef, and had got the people to submit to the overseer. A great many from all the villages came to receive the tools, and all without exception evinced a modesty, civility and respect, which surprized as much as it delighted me. Nothing more is heard about moving elsewhere."

In another letter, written a few days later, he recognizes that the discontent is not entirely dissipated, and relates bits of a conversation overheard by him between five Palatines sitting around a fire, who all

"agreed that the settlement at the Manor was a good plan (for the present). But they wanted more land. One counseled submission. Another said, 'We came to America to establish our families, and to secure lands for our children, on which they may be able to support themselves after we die. This we cannot do here.' One advised patience and hope. Another replied, 'Patience and Hope make fools of those who fill their bellies with them.' At this they all laughed and changed the conversation."

In several of the letters of Cast, Hunter and Secretary Clarke the statement is made that the discontent of the Palatines was due to malicious mischief-makers in the neighborhood. The last named wrote to the Lords of Trade :

"It 's hardly credible that men, who reap so great a benefit by these people, should be so malicious as to possess them with notions so injurious to themselves and prejudicial to her Majesty's interest ; and yet it is so. Great pains have been taken to magnify the goodness of that (land) at Schohary above this."

Little credit, however, can be given to this complaint. At the least, it is disingenuous. At that time that district was almost uninhabited and could furnish but few agents of disorder to this people, who needed no other influences than their own destitute condition and their defeated hopes.

The allusion in Cast's letter to the danger in settling Schoharie, was because of the immediate prospect of renewed hostilities with the French. The Schoharie valley was beyond the English settlements and, if occupied, would become the "most advanced frontier of the Province." While prudence required delay in going to that land of promise, there is notable evidence that fear and cowardice had little to do with that decision. The military returns of enlistment for the war from the Palatine villages show a remarkable readiness and devotion. From the three villages on the east side of the river went three companies, of one of which John Conrad Weiser was captain. The force of the three companies was one hundred and five men, fully one third of all the able-bodied men in the settlement. We need not follow their fortunes in the war. They were bloodless and involved little more than marching up to Albany and back again, the whole campaign of that year being a complete fiasco. But this large proportional enlistment of the Palatines proves the quality of the people, whom the authorities were endeavoring to subject to a state of vassalage, as very far above that low and squalid nature which some comments seem to intimate. They seem in this respect, whatever may have been the issue of the tar experiment, to have more than justified one of the hopes of the Lords of Trade, who coupled with their scheme for naval stores that of so planting the Palatines, that they should be "a barrier against the French and Indians and a defence to the Province." In the Hudson valley they nobly showed their manly spirit, and afterwards on

the Mohawk did yeoman's service in protect-
ing the liberties of their new country.

On the return of the volunteers the work
among the trees, in preparing them for the
production of tar, began again ; and with it
was again heard the voice of Palatine discontent, to which was added another item of complaint : that while the volunteers went willingly
to the war, "leaving their wives and little
children bare of necessities," they were not
paid for their military services. It is not at
all unlikely that the authorities regarded that
service, tho not in the contract, yet as con-
suming its time, fully paid for by the past expense of government on the Palatine account.
So early as in May the murmur among the
people had reached such proportions, that the
commissioners sent to New York for the Governor to come up to the Manor, when he found
on arrival a state of things not far removed
from mutiny. On inquiry of the people themselves, they told the Governor, that the lands
allotted to them on the Manor were good for
nothing, and demanded that he send them to
"Scorie,* to the lands given to the Queen for

* *Doc. Hist.*, iii, 396, 423.

them."   " They would rather lose their lives
than remain where they are. They had been
cheated by the contract, which was not the
same as that read to them in England. A great
many things promised them they had not received. The true contract they were willing
to perform, but to be forced by another contract to remain on these lands all their lives,
and work for her Majesty for the ships' use,
that they will never do." The Governor argued with them, and showed them the difficulties of settlement at Schoharie, that "they
would be compelled on that frontier to labor
as the Israelites did of old, with a sword in
one hand and an ax in the other."

With this the Governor pacified them for the
moment, and, thinking quiet to be restored,
set out on his return to New York ; but before
he reached the city, he was overtaken by a
messenger with the tidings that the mutiny
had broken out afresh. Whereupon he turned
back towards the Manor in no very amiable
frame of mind. An order was at once despatched to Albany for Colonel Nicholson and
a company of British soldiers ; and the Governor, getting the heads of the people together,

rated them soundly for their breach of contract, and demanded " how they dared to
disobey him." He had " the contract read in
High Dutch, and then asked, Would they
fulfil it ? that he might know what he should
do." At first, the people, cowed by the determined attitude of Hunter, replied that they
would fulfil the contract. But by the next
morning they had gathered courage and
changed their mind, and told the Governor
that they wished to go to Schoharie. Again
there was more argument and more threat
from the Governor, who dismissed the chiefs
of the people, with the order to think over
the matter and consult with their people, and
to give him a final answer on the morrow. By
the morrow the soldiers had arrived upon the
scene, and Hunter felt confident of subduing
the outbreak. Summoning the Palatine chiefs,
he demanded their final reply, and they answered with the same demand, " Scorie. They
would have the lands appointed for them by
the Queen." On this Hunter altogether lost
his patience. He in a passion stamped upon
the ground and said,* " Here is your land

* *Doc. Hist.*, iii., 424.

(meaning the almost barren Rocks) where you must live and die."

Meanwhile, as the "Deputies" were conferring with the Governor, the people took alarm from his evident anger and the presence of the soldiers. Some of the volunteers, who had been permitted to retain their arms, gathered and took their station not far removed from the Governor's quarters. They alleged that this movement was only for the protection of their chiefs, whom they supposed to be in danger, but the Governor was so incensed that he deployed the troops, and under threat of their fire disarmed the Palatines. This broke the spirit of the malcontents, who saw that further resistance was impossible. Forced to submit, they dispersed to their several villages, to wait until deliverance should come to them by another way.

Meanwhile they took up their task and wrought at it, if not contentedly, at least steadily, through the following summer, but now and then allowing some murmurs of discontent to escape them; while the Governor and the agents congratulated themselves on the progress made, and the glowing promise

of success "in this good and useful design."
There is no need for our following the course
of this work, now not far from a total and ig-
nominious failure ; but two quotations from
the correspondence of the summer may show
the highest point reached towards success.
Thus Sec'y Clarke wrote to the Board of
Trade in June : *

" The Palatines are now demonstrating sincere repent-
ance.   They are at work on the Trees, of which they
prepare fifteen thousand a day.   The children are busy
in gathering up Knots, which will be burnt this year, and
I doubt not a considerabe quantity of Tar made of them.
. . . The people work with all the cheerfulness
imaginable."

In September Hunter wrote :

" The tumults raised among them by the ill arts of
such as had a mind to crush the design, have had a quite
contrary effect, for since that time and a new modell of†
management, they have been very busy and obedient.
I have now prepared near a hundred thousand trees, and
in the fall will sett them to work on the second preparation.   That noe hands may be idle, wee imployed the
Boys and Girls in gathering knotts, out of which he

* *Col. Hist.*, v., 250.
† This refers to the putting Richard Sackett as Instructor in the
place of Bridger.

(Sackett) has made about 3 score barralls of good Tarr, and hath kills ready to sett on fire for as much more, so soon as he gets casks ready to receive it."

A curious and sharp comment on this last statement occurs in the reply of the Lords of Trade, who say : " We desire you to inform us how and out of what Funds those Casks are provided." To which the Governor answered that he had taken that cost out of the funds for the subsistence of the Palatines ! In another letter Hunter intimated that other necessities, such as the salaries of the agents, had been provided for out of that same subsistence fund, and one can easily conceive that the complaints of the Palatines as to quantity and quality of their food had abundant justification.

Towards the end of the fall it became evident that the Palatines had nearly reached the limit of their patience, and hints are frequent that the agents are meeting with increasing trouble. By an order of Hunter a court was established, " to regulate and govern the Palatines." The court had seven members, of whom were Livingston, Sackett, Cast, and "the Officer commanding the troops at the Living-

ston Manor." Evidently the people were of
such refractory spirit that the constant presence
of soldiers was necessary. In the following
spring Hunter ordered from Albany to the
Manor an additional force of "a Lieutenant
and thirty men." The coopers "are to be
kept to their work by as many soldiers as
needed." The court was to make the people
understand that, " by her Majesty's orders and
their own contract they are obliged to follow
the manufacturing of Naval Stores." It was
empowered to "punish by confinement or cor-
poral punishment, not extending to life or
mutilation ; and to take cognizance of all
Misdemeanors, Disobedience, or other Wilful
Transgression." * The List-Masters—of whom
Weiser was one—were to give to Sackett lists
of such men as were fit for any proposed work,
of whom Sackett " shall send for as many as
he please, and if they refuse they shall be punished." The court should meet " once a week,
or oftener, for punishing the delinquents. If
any of the people are negligent or Lazy," Mr.
Sackett is to "punish in such manner as he
shall judge fit." There would seem to be

* *Doc. Hist.*, iii., 401, 406.

small room for doubt that the Palatines were
held to a semi-slavery. However the terms of
the contract and the obligations incurred
through the outlay of the government could
rightly require the performance of the stipu-
lated work, the harsh, imperious, and cruel
proceedings of the authorities go far to justify
the Palatines in repudiating their share of obligation. A more faithful and kinder discharge
of the governmental obligations would have
met a much more docile mind. As it was, the
people considered themselves as cheated in
every way; neither money nor land promised
had been given; the food was not sufficient
or good; the clothing too scanty for comfort
or decency, while their superiors were to them
as hard taskmasters, whose rule was cruel and
oppressive. There is no room for wonder
that they were in a chronic state of revolt.

In such condition they entered upon their
second winter on the Manor, and in the cessa-
tion of their work upon the trees had plenty
of leisure to suffer, reflect and conspire.* In
the "Statement of Grievances," laid by them
before the King in 1720, they describe this

* *Doc. Hist.*, iii., 423.

winter in harrowing terms and language almost grotesque.   It was,

"very severe, and no provision to be had, and the people bare of Clothes, which occasioned a terrible Consternation among them, and particularly from the women and Children the most pitifull and dolerous Cryes and lamentations that have perhaps ever been heard from any persons under the most wretched and miserable Circumstances, so that they were at last, much against their wills, put under the hard and greeting necessity of seeking relief from the Indians."

This statement of relief from the Indians alludes to a deputation sent to the Indians of Schoharie, which did not go on its mission until the following autumn, and of which more will be mentioned hereafter.   It is probable that the resolution to send such deputation was made in the consultations of this winter of hardship, and waited a convenient season for putting it into execution.   It is evident that in these months they came to the decision to endure the miseries of their situation and the service, which they felt to be a bondage, no longer than necessity compelled.   Thus they came into the spring with a determination to resist and break away so soon as possible. The agents had a sorry time with them through the following months. In April, 1712, some of them deserted the Manor and crossed the river, seeking a refuge among the Dutch and their countrymen on the west side. Undoubtedly to check such desertion, the Justices of Kingston *—probably in response to a demand of Hunter or Sackett—ordered the constables "to take back to the Palatine villages any of the Palatines who have left and settled in sundry villages." The authorities were not minded that the Manor settlements should be diminished, or any of the Palatines should slip from underneath their hands. There is another curious token of this intention later in the year—made more curious by its accompanying the practical abandonment of the enterprise. The Governor, in writing to the commissioners at the Manor that the work must be suspended because of lack of funds, and giving permission to the Palatines to leave the Manor in search of occupation, forbids their going out of the New York and New Jersey provinces. "If any do, measures shall be taken for their

* *Doc. Hist.*, iii., 404.

rendition and punishment as deserters." Each
man leaving the Manor must obtain a Ticket
of Leave for a named place, a record of which
shall be kept, "so that if he abandon that
place he may be brought back and punished."
If any depart without a ticket, "apply to the
next Justice of the Peace for a Hue and Cry,
in order to pursue and bring him back, and
place him in confinement." *

The opening spring of 1712 found the
Palatines quite ready for any scheme which
would thwart the oppressive plans of the Governor. Not many notes are preserved, but
what little has been put on permanent record
shows that the difficulties of the undertaking
were increasing. Money to carry it on was
lacking, and the spirit of the people was becoming more and more obstructive. Sackett
builds a bridge over the Kill, " for the con-
veyance of Tar to the River side, and the
people say it will rot before it is put to that
use." †

The Governor's description of the situation
is very suggestive. ‡

*Doc. Hist., iii., 410.　　　†Doc. Hist. iii., 403.
‡ Col. Hist., v., 301.

"I employed," he wrote in January, 1712, "three hundred in the land forces. On return I disarmed them. They are planted where they are covered every way, and whilst they are armed they are ungovernable. What from the instigation of ill neighbors, and what from the natural turbulence of their temper, I find it hard to keep the generality of them to their duty and contract without force."

He claims that, despite such untoward circumstances, "the work is in great forwardness."

Later in the year he wrote with more hopefulness to the Lords of Trade: "Their work comes fully up to expectation. . . . I hear no complaints of late. The people work cheerfully since they understood that they should have one half of the profits of the manufacture." This arrangement was evidently a change in contract, introduced by Hunter himself to persuade the recalcitrant people. If such co-operative feature had been in the original contract, it is likely that more docility and more success would have marked the experiment.

In May the commissioners despatched a note to Colonel Ingoldsby, "Att the fort att Albany," in which they said, "finding that there is no good to be done with these people, who will obey no orders without compulsion, we desire your Hon^r to despatch s^d Detachment as soon as possible." Evidently, so far as the temper of the Palatines was concerned, the situation was becoming impossible of continuance.

Supplies were failing on account of lacking funds, and Livingston, who had the contract for furnishing bread and beer to the people, finds difficulty in carrying it on. There is a curious note of his to Lawrence Smith in New York, in which he complains of the difficulty in "supplying flower to the Palatines," and also insists upon his own advantage in not wanting any paper money, but hard silver. "Send it by first opportunity, els am quite untwisted." *

The contract was taken by Livingston from the date of the Palatines' arrival at the Manor. It demanded "for each person each day a quantity of Bread equal to ⅓ of a loaf commonly at price of 4½d. in New York, and one quart of Beer, such as is usually called Ship's Beer, of the price of £3 for each Tun-All." The bill rendered by Livingston for

* *Doc. Hist.*, iii., 391.

the first four months of such supply was
£5703–13–6.

As the summer of 1712 brought depletion of
funds the Governor sought to economize, and
wrote to Livingston that he should supply
"beer only for the men that work and not for
their families. I believe there are a great many
widows and Orphans among the people. I wish
I could know how many, that they might be
turned to some use, or be no longer a burden."*
The tone of this note and the somewhat cruel
suggestion at its close that, unless the widows
and orphans could be "turned to some use," they
must be turned adrift, make strong exhibit of
the sore financial straits into which Hunter and
his enterprise had come. In fact the financial
difficulties began before the first winter at the
Manor was over, and through the next year
and a half the Governor was put to all manner of hazardous measures to provide for the
prosecution of the work. By the end of that
period he came to the end of all his resources
both for patience and money. In September
of 1712 he wrote to Cast :

"I have exhausted all the money and credit I was

* *Ibid.*, p. 409.

master of for the support of the Palatines, and embarrassed with difficulties which I know not how to surmount, if my bills of exchange be not paid. . . . I have no desire that the people quit their establishments, now that the work has arrived at such a point of perfection." *

Then he proposed "this expedient," that Cast should call the people together, and tell them the state of affairs, and that they must shift for themselves. Those who can support themselves on the Manor should remain there. As to the others, "I wish they would accept any employment from farmers and others in this Province or New Jersey, until recalled by Proclamation or other notice. The contract is still binding and they *must* return on call." Then, after defining the police regulations already quoted, the Governor proceeds:

"I hope to have advices between this and spring of the payment of my bills of exchange, which will again enable me to support the whole of them. They must therefore not calculate on being dispersed for any greater length of time. . . . You see the necessity to which I am reduced. It causes me much uneasiness, because I am convinced that the work can not fail, were the people on the spot to prosecute it. I have the testimony of a good conscience in having done all that depended on

* *Doc. Hist.*, iii., 410.

me for their support and prosecuting the work for which they were destined."

This was the end of the experiment, a failure total and in some respects disgraceful. The Palatines so understood it, and more than half of them set out on their journey to "the promised land of Scorie," as will presently be detailed. To the Governor this large migration was both a grief and a displeasure. He wrote again to Cast:

"Do your best to retain as many as possible of these poor people within their duty, and I shall distinguish them from the rest by all the grants of land in my power. As to the others, I only pray God to turn away the Vengeance, which menaces them, and which they have richly deserved. Distribute as soon as possible whatever you have among the sick and indigent."

Inasmuch as the only Vengeance which menaced them was of the Governor's own invention, it does not appear that he need ask the Lord to turn it away.

In fact, the departure of this large company from the Manor seems to have ruffled and exasperated the Governor more than any other incident of the enterprise, and his after-conduct towards the Schoharie settlers was char-

acterized by a vindictiveness altogether without
excuse.   It is the only part of his relations to
the Palatines in which his conduct challenges
decided reproach.   It was also unlike himself,
as we understand his nature, and is only to be
explained by the intensity of his sense of disappointment on the failure of the " good and
useful design," which he had proposed to the
Board of Trade and had undertaken with ardor, in which he had sunk his entire fortune
and had taken on himself debts that he could
never meet.   Undoubtedly the Governor felt,
under the circumstances, that his honor was
specially involved, not only with regard to
financial obligations, but also as affected his
reputation as a man of affairs and as governor
of a province.   He wrote, while the work was
yet in progress, that from it he derived his sole
pleasure from his office ; and from the success
of the experiment he evidently counted on
reaping both distinction and wealth.   When
the disastrous failure ensued he felt that, in
place of becoming the object of great honor
as the man who had conferred signal blessings
on the Navy of England, he had rather become the butt for ridicule ; and, instead of re-

couping himself for his unwise advances—
unwise as too blindly trusting in the good
faith of the Home government—he had rather
plunged himself into a pit of irretrievable
bankruptcy. One can have sympathy for a
person in such circumstances, but at the same
time condemn his persecution of the Palatines,
whom he seems to have regarded as the sole
cause of the great failure.

The true cause of this failure should be
noted before following the Palatines who
sought the Schoharie. Among them is to be
placed the fact that the whole scheme was
based on a mistake as to material. It was
too easily taken for granted that the pines of
the Hudson could be made to produce tar
and pitch in such quantities as to bring re-
munerative returns for the pecuniary outlay.
This was a mistake and fatal to the enterprise.
Had there been no other obstruction, had the
Palatines been completely docile and unmur-
muring, had the English Treasury taken up
all of Hunter's bills and furnished all the
funds needed, still three or four years would
have demonstrated that the work could not
be prosecuted at a profit. The only recorded

return of the manufacture is of the "three score barrells of good Tar," which Hunter reports as made from the pine knots gathered by the children, concerning which we can be somewhat sceptical as to the quality of the product. Beyond this all the return is in promises and prophecies. Much stress is frequently and justly laid on the necessity for two years' "preparation of the trees," before the tar and pitch can be produced. This preparation is a peculiar process, by cutting and barking, through which the sap of the pine is concentrated. Then, after the proper length of time, the tree is felled and the wood burned in a kiln, in which the resinous gums flow out and the fibre is changed to charcoal. Up to the time of the breakdown the work had not gotten beyond the period of preparation, so that, except for the small amount of tar derived from burning the knots—which in all varities of pine have more or less of resin ready to hand, as one may say — there had as yet been no means of exhibiting the finished product. Hunter could write honestly, "the tar work was brought to all the perfection possible in the time."

There is in connection with this statement an amusing reply of Hunter to sundry critical "friends in England," who wished to "see some of the tar," and who, he says, "must take your Lordships' and my word for it." *

But neither their Lordships' nor Hunter's word could make tar and pitch in paying quantities from trees that did not produce them. The great tar-bearing tree of this continent is the *Pinus australis*, which is not found north of the southern borders of Virginia. Thence southward to the Gulf and within 150 miles of the coast it abounds in great forests, and is familiarly known as the Georgia Pine. So far as the Palatine immigration was concerned with the production of tar, if the North Carolina colony had been set to such work, the government might have looked for profitable returns. But the Hudson valley could not answer. The most common of the northern pines is the *Pinus Strobus*,—the ordinary white pine—much of which has almost no resin whatever, while none of it is rich enough in gum to make its burning an object. Besides this variety is the less common *Pinus rigida*,

* *Col. Hist.*, v., 347.

tho frequently found from Maine to Georgia. This tree is quite resinous, but does not grow to such size or occur in so large masses as to justify in any one spot so large expense as was involved in this attempt at tar-making by the Palatines.   There was, indeed, during the Colonial period—and may be down to this time—no little tar made in New England from the *Pinus rigida.** Williamson says, "Pitch and tar were made and exported in great quantities." But these "great quantities" must be understood as the aggregate of these products, made in small quantities and separate parts of the country, and constituting for the woodsman or farmer an avocation in the midst of his regular pursuits. This tree could not furnish the base for an extensive "plant" in any one place.

It seems somewhat strange that these facts were not sufficiently well known to prevent the undertaking. And yet the very fact of getting any tar at all from the northern pines might easily suggest to inexperience the thought, that much more would be produced by the larger number of people employed.

* *Hist. of Maine*, ii., 95.

Then, too, it is likely that neither Hunter nor the Lords of Trade knew any marked distinctions among the pines. In their minds, a pine was a tar-bearing tree, and that was about all they knew in regard to the matter.

It is also reasonably certain that, after his arrival in America, the Governor was misled by the man, John Bridger, whom he put into the place of Instructor to the Palatines.* This Bridger had been commissioned, some fifteen years before, by the Board of Admiralty to examine into the capacity of the American colonies for the production of naval stores—to survey the woods, and discover the forests most productive of material for masts, spars, tar and pitch. He went first to Barbadoes, and thence with Lord Bellomont to New York, in 1698. He was sent into New England to instruct its people in the process of tar-making; and on Hunter's coming with the Palatines was recalled to New York. He went with that people to the Manor, gave some instructions in the manufacture, began the "preparing" of some trees, and then returned to New England. In the following season Hunter wrote for him

* *Col. Hist.*, v., 175, note.

to resume his work among the Palatines. But Bridger refused to return, alleging various excuses to the Governor. He did not, however, tell him—what was probably his real reason— that the attempt being made on the Manor was hopeless from the start. It is probable that he early discovered the mistake made in that project, and so hastened to absent himself, either not wishing or not daring to enlighten the Governor as to the true state of facts. His refusal to return was the occasion of great anger on the part of Hunter, who lost very few opportunities for speaking of him in very disparaging words. "Ignorant, incompetent, unworthy, disobedient," are the best words which Sec'y Clarke can apply to him, while Hunter writes of his "wickedness and baseness," and with a fine scorn describes "his last letters, which denote a greater attention to his private profit than to the Publick Service." Bridger remained in New England, and was by the Massachusetts government made Surveyor-General of the Woods. In 1718 he was accused before the General Court of oppression and corruption, the charges being that he forbade the people felling trees fit for masts on their own lands, and then accepted bribes for permission so to do. On his trial he had the powerful protection of Governor Shute, and escaped conviction. The quarrel caused by the proceeding was very great, producing "difficulties which disturbed the province for a series of years," and in consequence of which, "at last the Governor was forced to leave the province." *

Had this mistake not been made, however, and had all the conditions, save the financial, justly promised a good success, the utter failure of monetary support was enough to wreck the enterprise. And for this, while reasons are plenty, there can be found no justification. In fact, the celerity with which the English government forgot all its engagements with Hunter, so soon as he and his Palatines were out of sight, and the nonchalance with which the Ministry treated their own pledges and Hunter's appeals, make a very curious record. The action of the English authorities was nothing less than a most unprincipled breach

* Williamson's *Hist. of Maine*, ii., 94.
Barry's *Hist. of Mass.*, ii., 109.
Hutchinson's *Mass. Bay*, ii., 222.

of faith, and a shameful abandonment of a worthy servant of the crown, who was faithfully endeavoring to carry out the instructions and orders of the government. Great as was his blunder in supposing that tar and pitch could be profitably made in the valley of the Hudson, he made a greater mistake in taking for granted that the Home government was composed of honest men.

The governmental advance of £8000, with which in hand he left England, was the last monetary outlay by the government on the Palatine account. But this amount was soon exhausted in subsisting the large body of that people on Nutten Island. Before their removal to the two Camps every penny was expended, and the Governor was compelled to use his personal fortune and credit towards their support. After having settled them up the river, he wrote to the Board of Trade :

"I hope your Lordships will think yourselves concerned to take care that what Bills I shall draw for their future subsistence, be duly comply'd with, lest by their failing the whole design prove abortive. . . . I am directed to subsist them at 6d. for all adult persons and 4d. for young persons, *per* day. . . . I compute that £15000 a

year for two successive years will be sufficient to defray
the expense." *

This, it would appear, included not only the
cost of subsistence, but also that of offices,
salaries and all contingent expenses.

As a matter of course, when the money advanced was expended, the Governor, in reliance
on the good faith of his superiors, made arrangement by bills of exchange for the immediate necessities.   He also spent in this service
his own entire fortune, confidently expecting
reimbursement from home.   Thus, with his
own money he bought the land from Livingston, and from the same source drew money
for the people's support, and from that time to
the end of the experiment all the money spent
in the work was of his providing, either from
his own purse, or from loans for the payment of
which he made himself responsible.   His bills
of exchange on London came back dishonored. ʼ
The British Treasury would have none of
them, and, so far as any record shows, never
repaid to Hunter a single penny of the enormous sums advanced by him for the support
of the enterprise.   The Governor's appeals

* *Col. Hist.*, v., 180.

we can give you.   It has not been possible to
do anything in that matter, this session of
Parliament."

Hunter's enemies in England used this opportunity to his great disadvantage.   Not only
did they succeed in obstructing the payment
of his bills, but also insinuated that he was un-
truthful in his representations about the work.
That he was mistaken in judgment is clear
enough, but there is nothing in the whole
transaction to show a lack of integrity on the
Governor's part.   On one occasion he grows
furious over these insinuations and writes to
Sec'y Popple:

"I have ordered Mr. Sackett and one of the Commissioners to go immediately to the woods, fell some of the
prepared Trees and bring them down hither—I mean the
loggs where the turpentine has settled—and I'll have
them burnt in the sight of the world, or exposed to
view, that I may not be imposed upon or be thought to
impose upon others."

Writing to Lord Stair in October, of 1715,
he recites the story of his efforts with the project, and describes " the recommendation of the
Lords of Trade for imploying 3000 Palatines
[as] turned into instructions by her Majesty's

letter, under her signet and sign manual," and avers that he had used such economy as to have saved £1500 a year out of the subsistence fund, to pay salaries and other expenses. "There is due to me upwards of £20,000. . . . Meanwhile I was left to beg my daily bread from a hard hearted Assembly here." Truly the poor Governor had an abundance of trouble,—and the most of it undeserved. It is reasonably certain that his motives were pure. No attack can be made on his integrity. Weiser, in speaking of the settlement of the people on the Manor, says that Hunter and Livingston delayed the consummation of the Queen's intention until land should come under their control, and "artfully and wickedly changed the course and destiny of the unsuspecting colony." This, so far as Hunter's purpose was concerned, may be set down to the not unnatural misjudgment to which the difficulties at the Manor would give rise in the mind of a Palatine.

Aside from the disastrous failure of the "great design to make tar for the Royal Navy," the administration of Hunter was with great honor and success. He took the

government in an ill time. The quarrels subsequent to the Leisler incident were still rife
and bitter. Not only the politics, but the
social life of New York, were rent by sharp
factional fights. Both parties vied in the
effort to win the special favor of the Gov-.
ernor, and Hunter's predecessors had erred in
yielding to such persuasions. He refused to
be drawn into the partisan strife, or to show
preference for either party. By such prudent
course, while "he found the province in a low
condition, he left it peaceful and prosperous.
Party spirit had been subdued and factions
were reconciled. He did more to quiet the
people than any, or all of his predecessors." *

Notwithstanding this wise management of
the Governor, he had a chronic trouble with
the provincial Assembly, on the question of
support both for himself and his administration. Long before his time the colonies had
learned impatience of dictation from England
or the royal governors, and quarrels were constantly in progress over the matters of taxa-
tion, impost and supply. Hunter's letters to
London abound with statements of these

* Schuyler's *Colonial New York*, ii., 63.

struggles, with here and there a flash of satire
on the colonial disposition. He writes:

" I acquainted them [the N. Y. Assembly] with your
Lordships' representation to her Majesty that the Palatines should, upon arrival here, be naturalized without
Fee or Reward, but they have declined it, for no reason
that I can guess but that it was recommended to them,
seeing they themselves were to be the chief gainers
by it." *

Sec'y Clarke describes this disposition of
the Assembly in similar caustic words, " He
[Hunter] has met with all the opposition and
discouragement which a people devoid of duty
and ripe with defection could give." In this
letter of Clarke is a reference to " the Tar-
work," which, in view of the issue of that enterprise and of the Governor's annoyances from
the Assembly, makes something of a demand
upon the reader's sympathy. The language
is:

" It is almost the only satisfaction his Excellency has
in this Province to see this great work goe on with that
promising success it does. . . He has the pleasure
of serving the best of Queens. That, therefore, and the
hopes of bringing this great affair of Pitch and Tarr
to perfection he must comfort himself with."

* *Col. Hist.*, v., 184, 250.

The Governor himself says, " It is some small comfort to me that I have brought the great undertaking to all the perfection that human power or industry could do in that time."

The complete collapse of the scheme, bringing the ruin of this only comfort to the Governor, already harassed to distraction by the political turmoil of the province, moves us to a compassionate mood. His experience in America had indeed a sad issue. He struggled on through nine years full of disappointment and burdens, to which in 1716 was added the death of his wife, a climax to his afflictions harder to bear than all the rest. In the year 1719 he obtained leave of absence and went to England, thinking that his personal presence could do much in defence against his enemies at home and in obtaining justice for himself. It does not appear that the government ever repaid him. He did not return to New York, but resigned his office and retired to private life. His character cannot fail to command respect, for generosity and conscientiousness. The not unnatural irritation of affairs, and especially the staggering blow of disappointment in the "great design of Tar," betrayed him into some actions not to be defended ; but for the most part he carried himself with admirable dignity and self-control. There is nothing finer in the *Colonial History* than his letter to Popple, written three years after the failure.* He reviews the Palatine ventures and, maintaining that there was no mismanagement on his part, says :

"About 13 Sep. 1712, I had certain advice that none of my bills would be paid, and then I stopt short, tho too late. . . All imaginable arts were used to stifle that project. I was sensible that I was struggling against a very *rappid* stream. But the interest of the Nation was so apparent, the reputation of those worthy Patriots who employed me was so much concerned, that I resolved to run all hazards, rather than have reason to accuse myself of having omitted any one thing in my power to bring it to perfection."

It was a great pity that "those worthy Patriots who employed" him were not equally careful for the reputation of their servant.

The extent to which Hunter had involved himself was, especially for that day, enormous. No full accounts are accessible, if extant ; but

* *Col. Hist.*, v., 447.

the bills presented by Livingston for subsistence are suggestive that the grand total of
expense was very large. The contract of
Livingston covered the period from the arrival
of the Palatines at the Manor, in Nov., 1710,
to the break-down in Sep., 1712. His bills,
presented quarterly, amount to £16,056-18-4
There are, however, three quarters, the bills
for which have not been preserved, but which
it is impossible to suppose were not presented. It is safe to add to the above amount
£10,000 for those three quarters. Besides
these large items a smaller one of £366-1-11½
represents his charges for "Salary" and
storage of provisions! Thus the whole sum
paid to Livingston must have been over
£26,000. In addition to this great sum the
Governor had other expense for the Palatines,
such as subsistence at New York, and transportation up the river—all of which he was
compelled to meet at private cost, after the
small advance from London had been exhausted. So it is evident that when he said
that "upwards of £20,000" were due him,
the real sum must have been largely in
excess of that amount.

This failure to support Hunter and this abandonment of the enterprise by the government were so remarkable, that the reader is made curious for the reasons of so atrocious bad faith. Fortunately, these reasons are not far to seek. There are two of them: one personal and the other political. Strangely enough the personal reason found its objective, not in Governor Hunter, but in Robert Livingston, who had sold the land for the Palatine settlement and had taken the contract for the supply of bread and beer. The method, by which a personal dislike of Livingston was able to reach so far as the ruin of a great enterprise and the bankruptcy of Governor Hunter, is somewhat curious.

When the bills given by Hunter came to London they were promptly presented by the Board of Trade to the Treasury for payment. But the Lords of the Treasury, instead of honestly meeting an expense authorized by the government, delayed payment until further advisement. This advisement was sought by Lord Dartmouth of the Treasury from the Earl of Clarendon, to whom he sent the statements of Hunter, desiring the opinion of the

Earl on the whole affair.* This resort to
Clarendon was doubtless because, in his chrys-
alis state of life as Lord Cornbury, he had
been Governor of New York. It was supposed that he knew enough of the province
and its forests to be able to advise. As it
happened, he knew Livingston and did not
love him, and was in no mood to approve anything which could issue to his advantage. Unfortunately, his dislike punished the wrong
victim, for Livingston got his money, and it
was the poor Governor who suffered. The
Earl replied to Dartmouth :

"I think it very unhappy that Col. Hunter, on his
first arrival, fell into so ill hands, for this Levinston has
been known many years in the Province for a very ill
man. He formerly victualled the forces at Albany, in
which he was guilty of most notorious frauds. He has a
Mill and Brewhouse upon his land, and, if he can get
the victualling of the Palatines, he will make a very good
addition to his estate."

The Earl argues that Livingston's lands are
not a good selection :

"Hudson's River *above* Albany, and Mohawks River,
Schenectady, are well known to be best." He objects

* *Col. Hist.*, v., 195.

that " the Bills drawn are computed on the numbers who landed at New York, of whom many are dead " [forgetful of the fact that these many had to be subsisted before they died]. "I am of the opinion that if the subsistence proposed be allowed, Levinston and some others will get estates, the Palatines will not be the richer, but will be confirmed in that laziness they are already too prone to, and will persuade themselves that they can obtain two years' more subsistence after the first two are gone."

He then goes on to ridicule the employment of the Palatines, and referring to the " Act for encouraging the importation of Naval Stores," says, "There was no fund provided for the payment of that reward, else that Act would have had a better effect than ten times the number of Palatines." So the Earl voided his hatred of Livingston in a letter sufficiently unprincipled, willing to sacrifice all other interests for the sake of thwarting that American baron. It had the effect intended in locking fast the treasury against all the appeals of Hunter and the intercessions of the Board of Trade.

The causes of Clarendon's bitterness against Livingston do not appear, nor is it easy at this late day to either justify or disprove his accusations. Certainly, Livingston was one of the ablest men of his time in the colony, a most shrewd man of affairs and capable of a vast amount of work. To his discredit it must be conceded that all his energies were turned towards his own benefit and aggrandizement, though it is not clearly shown that he was ever guilty of open dishonesty.* Born in 1654 in Ancram, Scotland, the son of a clergyman, he came to America when twenty years of age. He went to Albany, and in the following year was made Town Clerk and Secretary for Indian Affairs. He held this office for fifty years. In 1683 he married Alida Schuyler, widow of Rev. Nicholas Van Renssalaer, and in 1686 laid the foundation of his enormous estate, by obtaining the Patent to the Manor from Governor Dongan. He was a prominent Jacobite in the Revolution of 1688, and was driven from the province by the Leisler party. On the downfall of Leisler he returned and was restored to his offices, to which were added those of Collector of Excise and Quit Rents, Clerk of the Peace and Clerk of the Court of Common Pleas. He became associated with

---

* *Doc. Hist.*, iii., 434 note.

Bellomont and Captain Kidd, and thereby
added to his fortunes. In 1701 the Leisler party
returned to power in New York and called
on Livingston to account for large sums of
money, said to have passed through his hands,
and on his failing to comply, he was deprived
of his offices, and his estates were confiscated.
He fled to England, but on the voyage was
captured by the French and "treated barbar-
ously." At last released, he went to London
and obtained from the Queen a restoration of
his offices. He returned to New York in 1709,
became a member of Assembly, and in 1711
secured a repeal of the act confiscating his estates. He secured a seat in the Assembly for
his own Manor in 1716, and from 1718 to 1725
served as Speaker of that body. In 1721 he
resigned all his offices in Albany in favor of
his son Philip, and in 1726 retired from the
Assembly. Two years thereafter he died.
Evidently he was a man of so unique a per-
sonality and force, that these notes of his life
are quite in place here. Dr. O'Callaghan
sums up his story in these words :

"A man of unquestionable shrewdness, perseverance,
and large acquisitiveness. His main efforts, whether
13

in or out of the legislature, seem to have been directed principally to securing for himself wealth, office, and special privileges ; and every opportunity was seized by him to get the government and the legislature to recognize his Manor of Livingston."

He seems to have been an "ill man" to be associated with.　None of the royal governors, save Hunter and Dongan, could get on with him.　Those who had dealings with him were apt to find more or less of trouble, and even his friends spoke of him with a covert contempt. Bellomont * writes, in 1701, " I am told that Livingston has on his great grant of sixteen miles long and twenty-four broad, but four or five cottagers, men that live in vassalage under him, and are too poor to be farmers, having not wherewithal to buy Cattle to stock a farm." There was plainly something of a sting in the word " vassalage," as Bellomont designed it.

At the time of Hunter's arrangement with him about the Palatines it was openly said that "he would cheat the Governor.　But there appears no indication of such action in his accounts.　They are made with much particularity, such as a straightforward business

* *Col. Hist.*, iv., 822.

man would render, methodically, neatly, accurately." *

It is clear, however, that he had the best of the bargain and was the only man who received any benefit from the affair of the Palatines. In 1711, one of the agents at the Manor complained to the Governor of Livingston's grasping disposition, saying that he wanted to get into his hands the entire control of supplies, intimating also that he was endeavoring to undermine the Governor himself by whispers in high quarters and unfriendly messages sent to England. This aroused Hunter's wrath. Writing to General Nicholson, then in London, he speaks of Livingston's conduct as "base and villainous practice. . . . He is under many obligations to me, but I know him to be the most selfish man alive. If any man has any advantage by the Palatines being here, it is he." † By some means Livingston was able to appease the Governor's resentment, for we find them afterwards upon cordial terms. Whether Livingston was worthy, or not, of the condemnation of history, it is clear that the

* Schuyler's *Col. N. Y.*, i., 78.
† *Doc. Hist.*, iii., 405.

personal hatred of Clarendon towards him was a powerful, if not the most powerful, cause of the ruin of the Palatine experiment.

The other great cause of the failure obtaining in England was political. When Hunter and his Palatines left England the Whig administration, after a long lease of power, was already tottering, and before the expedition had reached America gave place to the Tories, who had no sympathy with the Palatines. In that age an incoming party did not have so much of conscience, as is supposed to exist today, about meeting the obligations incurred by its predecessors. Politcs was a fine game to play, however the country fared and whoever paid the piper. So, when these Tories came in, everything that the outgoing Whigs had done came up for review, criticism and, if possible, reversal. As it happened, the Palatine affairs made one great subject of criticism by the Tories. The Tory mind was, at the outset, affected against the cause of those refugees and opposed to the assisting hand of the government, and the following events very soon committed them strongly against the past sympathy and all future assistance.

Before the Palatines were embarked for the colonies, murmurs of jealous discontent on the part of the poor of London began to be heard. Says Burnet, * "Some things concurred to put the vulgar into ill humor : it was a time of dearth and scarcity, so that the poor were much pinched." The aid given to the Palatines "by the Queen and voluntary charities of good people filled our own poor with great indignation, who thought that these charities, to which they had a better right, were intercepted by strangers." The House of Commons, after the accession of the Tory government, "finding the encouragement given to the Palatines so displeasing to the people, ordered a Committee to examine into the matter."

The Report of this Committee has already been noticed. It was marked by much unfairness of judgment. The blame for the wholesale immigration was laid on the Naturalization Act of 1708, a measure passed by the Whigs after the arrival of Kockerthal with the first company from the Palatinate. There can be no doubt that the act was made because of that arrival, and with the hope of

* *Hist. Own Time*, iv., 230, 258.

attracting to England still larger numbers of
that distressed people.   The bill

"was debated in both houses with great vehemence.
The Whigs argued that it would be an effectual means
to encourage industry, improve trade and manufactures,
and repair the waste of men occasioned by the war.
The Tories objected with many dangerous consequences.
Spies and informers would come with the immigrants.
The strangers would insinuate themselves into positions
of trust, and would contribute to the extinction of the
English race.   They would greatly increase the number
of our poor, already so great a burden." *

It is a curious fact that, though this act was
undoubtedly passed to encourage the emigration of the Palatines, and though that people
came in crowds during the next year, yet it is
doubtful whether the act had anything to do
with that popular movement.   Very few of
the Palatines sought to be naturalized in London, and probably a still smaller number of
them were attracted thither by a knowledge
of that act.   The bait which drew them was
in the tidings of the kindness shown to Kockerthal and his companions, and in the prospect of being sent to America.   However, the
coincidence of the act with the immigration

* Mortimer's *England*, iii., 232.

gave the Tories a trenchant weapon for
attack upon the Whigs, and the House Committee made the most of it. Every objection-
able feature of the matter was emphasized and
exaggerated. "It happened," says Burnet,
"at a bad season. Bread was at double the
ordinary price. The time of sailing to the
plantations was at a great distance." The
sojourn in London was for eight months, with
constant accessions and the depletions made
by the Irish and Carolina settlements. During all this time the people were subsisted at
public cost. "The poor complained that such
charities went to strangers, when they needed
much . . . Some [Palatines] were both
inactive and mutinous, and this hightened the
outcry against them." The Tories made use
of all to discredit the Whigs. Smollett (*History of England*, ii., 101, 102) says:

"The inhabitants of St. Olaves and other parishes presented a petition, complaining that a great number of
Palatines, inhabiting one house, might produce a contagious distemper, and in time become a charge to the
public, as they were destitute of all visible means of
subsistence. This petition had been procured by the
tories, that the House of Commons might have another
handle for attacking the late ministry."

They managed to bring the House to a sudden vote that the Palatines were

"an extravagant and unreasonable charge to the Kingdom, and a scandalous misapplication of public money, tending to the increase and oppression of the poor, and of dangerous consequence to the constitution of Church and State, and whoever advised their being brought over was an enemy to the Queen and Kingdom."

The repeal of the Naturalization Act took place in 1712. The former vote of condemnation was taken in 1711, while the work on the Manor had just begun, and Hunter was already pressing for payment of his advances. To the official mind in England the entire undertaking was thus thoroughly discredited, and all its obligations were repudiated, without regard to the good faith of government or the pitiable plight of the New York Governor. It may be that, after his return to England, Hunter obtained some redress from a later administration ; but no record thereof is found in the colonial documents, nor would it be likely to there obtain statement.

CHAPTER VI.

THE PROMISED LAND.

THE letter from Hunter to Cast, written in September, 1712, saying that he had "exhausted both substance and credit," gave the finishing stroke to the "great and good design." Nor was the work ever resumed. The cost of it was accounted as so much money thrown away. At sundry times, through the remainder of Hunter's government of the province, references to the scheme were made in the correspondence with the Board of Trade. The Governor laments over the failure and never loses his confidence that a noble and most beneficent success would have been achieved, had the effort been properly supported. At one time the Lords of Trade were stirred to languid interest in the subject, and inquired of Hunter as to the condition of the

trees already prepared, and the prospects of
any new engagement in the work.   Their letter came to Hunter as the breath of hope, and
was responded to with some enthusiasm.   He
replied :

" Since your Lordships have hinted an intention to resume the project, in this Province there is Pitch Pine
trees enough to yield a quantity of stores sufficient for
the uses of all the Navigation of England.   .   .   .   One
of the Commissioners has returned.   He has brought
along with him some chips cut by him from several of
the prepared trees, by which I may reasonably compute
that about a third of the Trees will yield well.   .   .   .
I can think of no solid way of preventing the total de-
cay of trade, and consequently the ruin of the Provinces,
but by setting on foot and carrying on vigorously the
production of Naval Stores mentioned."

The Governor's hope certainly dies hard.

In his next letter on the subject, however,
he tunes a more dolorous note.   Under date
of October 2, 1716, he wrote :

" I am at a loss for the true cause of the disappointment
from the Trees prepared for tar.   What I chiefly guess
to be the cause of this miscarriage is this, that the Trees,
being barked by an unskilful and unruly multitude, were
for the most part pierced in the inward rind, by which
means they became exhausted by the sun's heat in the
succeeding summer.   Many of them are good, but not
in that quantity that will answer the expence and labor."

Then he reiterates his former statements as to the vast capabilities of the province for this production, and concludes, "but after the disappointment I have met with, I cannot advise the renewing of the project until we have persons skilled and practiced." This reads like an epitaph and moves one to sympathy with the Governor in this burial of his most cherished hope, out of which, he tells us, he had taken more comfort than from aught else in his government in America. But this is the end, and we read no more of naval stores as the expected product of New York.

Meanwhile the Palatines on the Manor recognized their freedom, and at once took steps towards making of it the best use possible. There are no records of any general plan of action, but subsequent events would indicate that the disposition of the entire company was outlined in council. Some were to stay on the Manor—a little less than one third of their number—and make for themselves permanent place ; seeking subsistence from the soil and from hiring themselves to neighboring farmers. Among this number also were those—women and infirm—who did not esteem themselves

equal to further migration and to new struggles with unknown conditions.   The rest of
the people girded themselves for their journey
to "the promised land of Scorie."

Of the quota remaining on the Manor not
many notes need here to be made.   They
settled down to farming and such other voca-
tions as were needed, and were the fathers
of a like permanent and sturdy stock to that
which for generations has peopled the lands on
the west side of the river.   There appears in
the Documentary History (iii., 421), under
date of 8 Oct. 1715, a petition to the Governor
from John F. Hager, on the part of himself
and sixty families of the Palatines on the
Manor, asking "license to build a church in
Kingsbury, 60 feet in length and 40 feet
wide, to Perform Divine Service, according to
the Liturgy and Rites of the Church of England as by Law established . . . also
liberty to Crave the favour and charity of well-
disposed People for aid and assistance."   Inasmuch as this Hager was himself a clergyman—
either Lutheran or Reformed, to which two
forms of the Protestant faith all the Palatines
adhered—it is probable that the stipulation as

to the Church of England was designed and understood as merely a legal fiction. Whatever action was taken by the Governor on this petition, the church contemplated could not have been erected, for in 1721 Governor Burnet, who succeeded Hunter in the province, issued a brief to Robt. Livingston, permitting him "to make collections for preparing or building a church on his Manor, and to call a Pious Reformed Protestant Minister from Holland." This was the beginning of the still existent Reformed Church of Germantown.

Another interesting item, is found in a " Petition of Jacob Sharpe, Christophel Hagatorn and Jacob Shoemaker, in behalf of themselves and other Palatines on the Livingston Manor," asking for a grant to them and their heirs of the lands purchased by Governor Hunter from Livingston. This petition bears date of June 13, 1724, and to it the Council replied by directing the Surveyor-General, Cadwallader Colden, to inquire what families, and how many, were on the land and willing to take His Majesty's grant. He presently reported the number of families as sixty-three, "not all having a like quantity in possession," and recommended that it was "wise to grant the said land " to the petitioners named and other principal men, *in trust* for the whole company. Inasmuch as this land belonged to Hunter, who paid good money for it out of his own purse, one is moved to wonder if any compensation was made to him therefor. The land seems to be regarded as tho, by his departure from the province, it had escheated to the crown. It does not appear, however, that the advice of Colden was followed by the Assembly, nor do we here need to inquire farther about it.

About thirty families on the Manor moved a few miles southward and settled on lands covered by the patent given to Henry Beekman. It is said—a statement difficult to verify—that their movement was due to Livingston's unwillingness to give them titles to the lands occupied by them. He did not wish to alienate the fee, and would only agree to a lease for three lives. This, of course, must refer to such of the people as had sought a freehold outside of the tract purchased by Hunter, unless Livingston, after Hunter's departure, had attempted to assert a right over that tract.

These thirty families found a more liberal disposition in Henry Beekman, who sold them lands in fee, in that part of his patent which is covered by the town of Rhinebeck. The name of that town is distinctly Palatine, as in its first syllable a memorial of the much-loved river in the old country. As the last syllable was formerly written, "beek," it has been thought to have been taken from the name of Beekman, in honor of his fair dealings with these people.

｜Whatever may have been the difficulty on the land question, or the origin of the latter half of "Rhinebeck," it is certain that that town was founded by these Palatines, many of whose names still obtain in the locality. From Rhinebeck also the descendants of these people found various and scattered homes throughout Dutchess County, and have given to the State and nation many men of prominence and usefulness.

Those of the people who went to the Schoharie valley had for several years an experience of further affliction. Some writers have charged these troubles to their ignorance ; but beyond denial the origin of them is found in the anger of the Governor and the cupidity of designing men, to whom the Governor, in the first heat of his resentment, surrendered them as victims. The chief man among them, John Conrad Weiser, educated and an ex-magistrate, cannot be reckoned as an ignorant person. However "riotous and rebellious" he may have been in resisting the Governor and his agents, he was not likely to sacrifice the interests of his people through sheer ignorance of common law.

As already noted several times in this narrative, the thought of the supposed original destination of the Palatines had not lost its charm to the minds of very many of them. To all remonstrances and arguments of the Governor and Cast they answered with one word—Schoharie. They called it, "Schorie." This to them was the land of promise. They talked of Schorie; they dreamed of Schorie, and to Schorie would they go. In their last winter on the Manor they had planned for ways to reach that country of blessing, and through the following spring and summer waited for fitting opportunity to put their plans in operation. They must proceed with caution, as

any general or large migration, while the tar-
work was in progress, would be promptly
checked by the military kept at the Manor to
compel the submission of the people. Even
individual deserters were brought back and
punished.

Thus waiting, they hailed the order to cease
the work and for the people to shift for themselves, as a proclamation of freedom. They
at once despatched to Schoharie seven deputies—principal men among them—and the '
" List men," of the villages, of whom Weiser
was chief. These men were to visit the valley,
examine its land, deal with the Indians in the
neighborhood, and find the best route for the
people to take thither. The visit of these
deputies must have been made in the early
fall, and according to their own report they
were received by the Indians in the valley with
the utmost friendliness.

Brown * says—a statement probably drawn
from tradition, for he gives no authority—that
the first inhabitant of the Schoharie valley was
a French Indian, Karigondonte, who had married a Mohawk squaw, in consequence whereof

* *Sketch of Schoharie*, p. 52.

14

he was forced to leave his tribe. He took pos-
ession of the Schoharie valley and seems to
have established there a sort of Cave Adul-
lam, attracting thither from the surrounding
tribes " such as were discontented and such as
were in debt." Presently, he had gathered
about him " a nation three hundred strong,"
which took the name of their chief, and was
made up of Mohawks, Mohegans, Discororas,
and Delawares.

That section of the valley occupied by these
Indians and given to the Palatines, afterwards
described as the Schoharie Flats,

"begin on the Little Schoharie Creek, in the present
town of Middleburg, at the high-water mark of the Schoharie river, and at an oak stump burned hollow—which
stump is said to have served the Mohawk and Stockbridge Indians as a corn-mill—and ran down the river
to the north, on both sides, a distance of ten miles, and
containing about twenty thousand acres. By the side of
this stump was erected a pile of stones, still standing after
1800. Upon the stump were cut the figures of a turtle
and a snake, the sign of the Karighondonte tribe, as a
seal of the contract."

Sims,* from whose history the above quotation
is taken, represents this contract as one made

* *Hist. of Schoharie Co.*, p. 47.

by the Indians with "an agent of the Queen,
to prevent hostilities between them and the
Germans." This, as we know, is a mistake.
No agent of the Queen made such a contract.
On the contrary, all the Queen's representatives
in the province, who had any relation to the
matter, did their best to prevent the Palatines
going to Schoharie, and, after they had gone
thither, to render residence there as uncomfort-
able as possible. If there was any such stump
and any seal of contract engraved thereon, the
"party of the second part" must have been,
not the Queen's agent, but the Palatine deputies from the Manor.

These seven "Chiefs,"—as they are termed
in some parts of the narrative,—headed by
Weiser, proceeded on their mission by way of
Albany, and there obtained an Indian guide.
He led them over the Helderbergs and down
the Fox Creek to its junction with the Schoharie, in the very heart of their chosen valley.
Entering it in the early fall, they must at once
have realized that their dreams had not played
them false, for certainly fairer sight their eyes
had not beheld since they left their old country
on the Rhine. It is a deep valley, where the

copious dews from April to October make a constant and luxuriant verdure.   The hills on either side, here sloping gently upward, and there standing in bold bulk of precipitous rock, seemed to promise bulwarks of defence and protection from further foes.   The broad alluvial flats prophesied plenty on the farms that were to be, while the river, like a broad silver ribbon, wound its way among the level meadows, its full and quiet flood an image of contented peace.

The Palatine statement tells of most hospitable treatment of the deputies by the Indians. The deputies "intreated them [the Indians] to give 'em permission to settle on the tract of land called Schorie."   This the Indians readily granted, saying that "they had formerly given this land to Queen Anne for them." This last statement provokes a smile, for whatever may be the truth about that gift to the Queen, it is pretty certain that the company of Karigondonte had nothing to do with it. However, he and his nondescript tribe seem to have had the friendliest disposition.

When the deputies returned to the Manor and made report of the welcome extended, "it put the people in heart. All hands fell to work, and in 2 weeks' time cleared a way thro' the woods of 15 miles long, with the utmost toyle and labour." The locality of this "way thro' the woods" is somewhat uncertain, tho it is probably to be found near the end of the journey, and not at the beginning, as the narrative would imply. The unbroken wilderness, through which the pioneer's axe must make a road, was rather on the Helderbergs than on the bank of the Hudson. The migration of the people was in two companies. The first company was composed of fifty families, which, so soon as possible after the return of the deputies, set out upon the journey. Whether they travelled by boats to Albany or trooped the way on foot the "statement" does not tell. It was doubtless a sorry-looking company and poorly furnished, appealing in the poverty of their resources to the charity of the good people of Albany. And in the immediately subsequent months, their need received much help, not only from the Dutch in Albany, but also from the Consistory of the Dutch Church in the city of New York.

Hardly was the toilsome journey over before

a new and different trouble began, the tale of
which beginning may best be told in their own
words :

" Being arrived and almost settled, they received orders
from the Gov.ᵒᵘʳ not to goe upon the land, and he who
did so should be declared a Rebell. . . This Message
sounded like thunder in their ears and surprised them
beyond expression ; but having seriously weighed matters amongst themselves, and finding no manner of like-
lihood of subsisting elsewhere,but a Certainty of perishing
by hunger, cold, etc., if they returned, they found themselves under the fatall necessity of hazarding the Govᵐ Resentment, that being to all more eligible than Starving.*

|It does not appear why the Governor should
have sent this order, or have had any just
`objection to the settlement in Schoharie.
Certainly, in his message abandoning the " tar-
work," he had told the people to shift for
themselves, and had only limited their choice
of location to the two provinces of New York
and New Jersey. He had, indeed, required
that those who left the Manor should obtain
tickets of leave, and this formality, probably,
the people did not observe. Nothing, however, is said about such dereliction, tho it is clear

* *Doc. Hist.*, iii., 425.

that the people departed without asking the Governor's permission to go to Schoharie. The whole aspect of the movement to his mind was of a refractory body withdrawing from under his immediate eye and authorty, and going behind the barriers of forest into a retired valley, whither the obligations of the contract could not easily follow them. He was apprehensive lest, if that precious project should be resumed, he might not be able from that distance to bring his workers. Besides, and fully so powerful, was a sentimental consideration : that for two years that "tract of land called Schorie" had been as a bone of contention between him and the Palatines. They, like Israel in Egypt, had been incessantly crying, "Let us go ; " and he as constantly replying, "I will not let you go." And now the Governor saw himself outwitted, more by the hardness of events than by the cunning of the people ; and yet, however brought about, a thing to be resented. There was much injustice in the Governor's thought, and more in his subsequent conduct, and yet it is quite intelligible that, with all his soreness of spirit over the great failure, and his irritation at the

self-determined methods of the Palatines, he
should resolve that, whatever happened, they
should not possess that coveted valley.

But for the present he was powerless. The
first band of the emigrants had reached the
Schoharie, and the winter had closed in upon
them. Nor in any case could the Governor
drive them out by force. We shall see that
he adopted other means, far more worrying.

) In the meantime the settlers suffered many
privations through the winter. The "barbar-
ous people showed them no little kindness,"
and out of their own scanty stores of maize
gave freely to them. Young Weiser writes:
" They broke ground enough (in the spring)
to plant corn for the use of the next year.
But this year our hunger was hardly endura-
ble." The Indians showed them where to find
many edible roots. " Many of our feasts were
of wild potatoes (oehmanada) and ground-
beans (otagraquam)." In the opening spring
the other company, about one hundred families, made their way to the valley. The quaint
narrative says:

" In the same year in March (1713) did the remainder
of the people (tho treated by the Governor as Pharaoh

treated the Israelites) proceed on their journey, and by God's Assistance travell'd in [a] fourtnight with sledges thro' the snow, which there covered the ground above 3 foot deep, cold and hunger, Joyn'd their friends and countrymen in the promised land of Schorie."

This comparison of Hunter to Pharaoh may allude to some unrecorded actions of the Governor by which he essayed to detain the people on the Manor.   If so, the determined migration served to add to his resentment.   He had time to lay his plans while the people made their settlements.

They disposed themselves in seven villages— dorps or dorfs—along the Schoharie, naming each from one of their seven chiefs.   Of these the more considerable were Weiser's dorp, in the present Middleburgh ; Fuchs's dorp (afterwards anglicized to Fox), at the junction of the Fox Creek with the Schoharie ; and Kniskern's dorp at the mouth of the Cobleskill. On the site of the present Court House village was an eighth hamlet called Brunnen dorp, from the springs in the hill-side, and from which the hamlet was afterwards called Fountaintown. At Fuchs's dorp was the centre of the settlement.   On the Fox Creek was built the first mill which freed the people from carrying their grain to Schenectady. It was at the Fuchs's dorp that the people gathered for Sunday worship ; and on the sightly bluff, which divides the Fox from the Schoharie, was, in 1772, built the Old Stone Church—or Fort—which still stands, one of the most picturesque historic buildings in the State.

The people had not long been in Schoharie and were still suffering through the privations incident to their new settlement, when the first of their troubles about their lands was put upon them by the son of the Colonel Nicholas Bayard, who, about twenty-five years before this time, had received from Governor Fletcher a patent to a "certain tract of land called Skohare, beginning at the mouth of the Skohare river and runs to head of said river." * Inasmuch as the Schoharie is about fifty miles long, this Bayard patent may well be rated among the "extravagant grants" given by Fletcher.† Colden describes this governor's " liberal hands, with which he gave away lands. The most extraordinary favors of former governors were but petty grants in comparison with his." We

* *Col. Hist.*, v., 634.   † *Doc. Hist.*, i., 250.

are not to understand that these grants by
Fletcher were given without "a consideration." He was notoriously corrupt.* Bellomont wrote, in 1701, "I believe not less than
seven millions of acres were granted in thirteen
grants, and all uninhabited except Mr. Rans-
lear's." He said also that Fletcher had made
a fortune of £30,000 by his corrupt practices.

The London Board of Trade was alarmed
by this extravagance of Fletcher and laid the
matter for advice before the Lords Justices of
England, who declared such grants improper
and that they should be annulled. Bellomont
was instructed to obtain from the provincial
Assembly an act voiding all the grant patents
issued by Fletcher. As already noted, such
act was passed in 1698, and Colonel Bayard lost
his immense estate. On several occasions efforts were made to get this act repealed—and
several petitions of Samuel Bayard are preserved, requesting to be restored to his father's
lands.

What this Bayard expected to realize among
the Palatines is not quite clear, but there can
be no doubt that his scheme was not charged

* *Col. Hist.*, iv., 822, 826.

with beneficence to the new settlers. Sims and others speak of him as "an agent of the Queen." Their account runs that he came to Schoharie and published a notice "to every householder, who would make known the boundaries of land taken by him, that he would give a deed in the name of the Sovereign." * The statement is absurd. Bayard could not have been an agent of the Queen. He was not in government favor in the province, and had no relations to the government in England, while all the properly accredited agents of the Queen and the home government were distinctly unfriendly to the Palatines and in no mood to arrange that their titles to the Schoharie lands should be made clear. The story quoted proceeds to say that the Palatines were enraged at Bayard, supposing that he had come in the interest of their oppressors, and mobbed him, driving him out of the valley; that he went to Schenectady, and thence sent back a message to Schoharie, "offering to give to such as should appear there with a single ear of corn, acknowledge him as royal agent, and name

* Sims, *Schohairie Co.*, p. 60.

the bounds of it [their land], a free deed and lasting title." It appears that Bayard's patience and generosity were extensive after such treatment as he had received. But they were not proof against the contemptuous refusal of the Palatines to take any notice of this offer, for the tale concludes that, since nobody from Schoharie appeared to take advantage of his kindness, he went to Albany and sold the lands to Myndert Schuyler, Peter van Brugh, Robert Livingston Jr., John Schuyler, and Henry Wileman. These gentlemen did, indeed, come into possession of titles to Schoharie, but not by means of such purchase from Bayard.

The reflection upon this story by those who record it for sober history is that the hostile action of the Palatines was due to their ignorance, in consequence of which they deprived themselves of secure titles and brought on all their subsequent troubles. But we may set that aside as quite impossible, for Weiser and the chiefs were intelligent men, and undoubtedly judged correctly that Bayard's mission was not of a friendly nature, and that any titles taken from him would be of no value.

It is far more probable that, in place of offering
them titles from the Queen, Bayard planned
to practise upon their supposed ignorance, and
on the ground of his father's annulled patent
to induce them to either buy or take leases
from himself. Nor can we suppose that the
" Gentlemen of Albany," who were afterwards
called the " Five Partners," were ignorant
enough to buy from Bayard land which had
been taken from him by legislative enact-
ment. They took their title from under the
hand of Gov. Hunter, tho it may be that
the suggestions of Bayard had something to
do with their application.*

Bayard had not long disappeared from the
valley, when another claimant to Schoharie
lands came on the scene, in the person of
Adam Vroman, of Schenectady. The land
to which he had title was situated well up
the valley, embracing the most of what is
now the township of Middleburgh. His
patent is still outlined on the county maps,
and he has a more enduring monument in

* This Bayard was in some way connected with the Leisler Rebellion in New York, was tried for high treason and condemned to
death, but was pardoned. Cornbury declared that the action against
him was very unjust (*Col. Hist.*, iv., 974).

the name of one of the mountains at its side, a bold, high, and rocky headland, called Vroman's Nose, jutting out into the Flat and dominating the valley for miles, both south and north.   He is said to have purchased his lands from the Indians in 1711, but his chief reliance for title rests on the patent given by Gov. Hunter in August, 1714—a date eighteen months later than the Schoharie migration of the Palatines.

Vroman came to take possession of this land in the year after the issuance of the patent, and had a rather hard time of it, as appears from his complaint to the Governor.   We can let him tell his story in his own words, which were written at Schenectady, "9 July 1715. In hast."   He writes, " The Palatines threatened in a rebellious manner, if I should build or manure the Land at Schore that your Excellency was pleased to grant me a Patent for."   He had manured and sowed some of the land, and " they still drove their horses on it at night."   He was

" building a stone house 23 feet square and so high so I had Layd the Beames of the Chamber, they had a Contryvance to tie bells about horses' necks and drive them to and fro. In which time they pulled my house Stones and all to the Ground. . . . They used such rebellious expressions that was never heard of. . . . John Conradus Wiser has been the Ring Leader of all factions. . . . They made the Indians drunk to that degree to go and mark off land with them. . . . I am no wayes secure of my life. They went and pulled my son off of the waggon and beat him and said they would kill him or his father or any body else who came their. . . . Wiser and two or three more has made their escape by way of Boston and have said they would go for England, but has left his Son which is their Interpreter to the Indians and every day tells the Indians many Lyes, whereby much mischief may ensue more than we now think off and is much to be feared . . . I don't find a Great many Concerned with this Wiser and his son in their disobedient, unlawful, and Rebellious proceedings . . . Those that are good subjects among them and will not Joyn with them are afraid the others will Burn their houses down by their threatening words."

They must have been hot words indeed.

One can have considerable compassion for Vroman in this evil case, without at the same time condemning very severely the conduct of Weiser and his companions. Their proceedings were, of course, irregular and unlawful, but they were the only means left to them for defending what they not unjustly considered

their rights. They knew that no complaints
of invasion on those rights would be entertained by the Governor for a moment. They
perceived that the Vroman patent was but one
item in a plan to deprive them of all hope of
possession in their promised land. So in the
absence of any friend at court, without any
legal title to the land they had occupied, but
which they believed to be morally their own,
they adopted the policy of worrying and fright-
ening off the intruders. It was a weak policy,
but all they could adopt. Nor did it succeed.
The Dutch blood of the Vromans had too
much staying quality for that.

One other measure, indeed, they did attempt
—a purchase on their own account from the
Indians. Their "statement of Grievances"
relates that, when some people from Albany
endeavored to obtain land "round them so as
to close them up," they themselves "bought
the rest of the land at Schorie, being woods,
Rocks and pasturidg, for 300 pieces of eight."
This is the transaction to which the complaint
of Vroman alludes, "getting the Indians drunk
so as to mark off land with them." The
younger Weiser speaks of this purchase for

15

three hundred dollars, as tho that sum were
paid for the entire valley, and on the visit of
the deputies to the Indians.

But neither this purchase not the persecution of Vroman aided them.   They were evidently the victims of the Governor's resentful
purpose to leave them not a foot of ground to
stand upon in Schoharie.   There is no injustice
to Hunter in so speaking.   However incon-
sistent with his general character this conduct
of the Governor was, it yet finds plenty of evidence.   Beyond question the right thing for
him to have done under the circumstances was
to give to the Palatines land in Schoharie.
They had come over under a contract, part of
which promised to them land, and the failure
of the tar project through no fault of theirs
did not absolve the government from its promise to give them forty acres for each family.
Besides, whatever may have been the foundation in fact for the Palatine dream of Schoharie, it is certain that others than themselves
considered that valley as their destined place.
Hunter himself admitted this, but alleged the
difficulty of tar-making in that locality as a
reason for settling them on the Hudson.

When, therefore, that design was abandoned, and a large majority of the Palatines had found their way to Schoharie, the only proper thing for Hunter to do, was to confirm them in possession, if not of the whole valley, at least of so much acreage as would satisfy the conditions of the contract.

But the fact was that the Governor did not exercise a judicial mind. He seems to have visited on the poor Palatines all his wrath because of the great failure, for which they were in no wise to blame. He should have visited his anger on the British Treasury; and on Clarendon, who involved Hunter in his hatred of Livingston ; and perhaps on Livingston, who may have cheated him and certainly did get all the profit there was in the business for anybody. The Palatines he should have acquitted of blame and settled them peacefully and undisturbed. Instead, he pursued a course alike reprehensible and unworthy of himself. Perhaps it would not be correct to say, that the course of events, by which the Palatines found settlement at Schoharie difficult and more than half of them were driven from the valley, was in consequence of any prearranged plan of the Governor. At the same time it is clear enough that he did not hesitate to embrace the opportunity offered by the cupidity of land-grabbers to make his spite against that people effective. This situation is well expressed by E. M. Smith—the only writer who seems to have formed a correct judgment of these transactions—in his *History of Rhinebeck*. He there says : *

"There was evidently a purpose, favored by Gov. Hunter, that the land of Schoharie, which they claimed and whither they had gone, should not be owned by these people, but that it should be owned by some non-resident favorites, perhaps for a personal consideration, to whom they should for ever remain mere 'hewers of wood and drawers of water.'"

This conclusion is fully justified on careful comparison of dates. Thus the voiding of the Bayard grant took place in 1698, from which time, whether with or without the ground of an Indian gift, the lands were looked upon as belonging to the Queen. Until the entrance of the Palatines in the late fall of 1712, no white man had attempted possession and no claim of ownership had been asserted, unless

* p. 91.

we except the possible purchase from the Indians of a portion of the lands by Vroman in
1711. On any right so acquired, however, it
is significant that Vroman himself does not
lay stress, but founds his title on the patent
given by Hunter in the summer of 1714. This ·
was a year and a half after the Palatines had
gone to the valley. * The Vroman patent
covered the lands of Weiser's dorp, and also
those of Ober-Weiser's dorp, another hamlet
soon established at a little distance up the
stream. There is not much of detraction from
the sinister quality of this grant in the fact
that Vroman's petition for the grant was
made a year before the patent issued. That
also was subsequent to the Palatine occupation, by several months ; and one needs not
to draw severely on imagination to suppose,
that the Palatine entrance was the means of
turning the attention and cupidity of Vroman
towards Schoharie. But, however that may
be, there is no doubt that Hunter gave to
Vroman lands which he knew were already in

* For dates of Petitions and Patents for Land, here alluded to,
see "Calendar of N. Y. Land Papers," pp., 142–182. The Papers are
in vols. v.–x., of " Land Papers " in the office of the Secretary of
State.

possession of the Palatines. To suppose that
Vroman paid him for the lands, as the Palatines were unable to do, is only to add the
charge of corruption to that of cruelty. The
only pecuniary condition for a patent allowed
by law was the payment of an annual Quit
Rent to the crown, whatever may have been
done by way of purchase from the Indians.
Hunter was an honest man, and we cannot
suppose him guilty of those practices which
disgraced his predecessor, Fletcher. Undoubtedly, beyond extinguishing the Indian title,
and the clerical fees, Vroman paid nothing for
his patent. As to the necessary Quit Rents,
the Palatines would have engaged for those
as readily as he. There can be no reason,
save that of the Governor's pleasure, for the
preference of Vroman to the Palatines. Vroman did not attempt to enter on possession
until more than two years after the people
had settled on the lands.

But this is not all. Whatever may have
been the nature of the transactions between
Bayard and the "Five Partners," those gentlemen did not consider their title secured,
save by a patent from under the Gov-

ernor's hand. Their petition was presented
in May, 1714, and the patent was issued in
the following November. " The patent began
at the northern limit of Vroman's patent on .
the west side, and at the Little Schoharie kill
on the east side, and ran north on both sides
of the river to beyond the Coble's Kill." *
This finished the legal expulsion of the Palatines begun by the Vroman patent. The two
patents together granted away from them the
ground upon which they had built their houses
and every foot of land which they had broken
for seed. The action would seem to justify
the language of Weiser, " as the hawk pounces
on the dove cote, these powerful parties fell
on the victims."

There appears under date of the same
November a license to " Samuel Staats and
Rip Van Dam to purchase 2000 acres each at
a place called Foxes Creek in the county of
Albany." Foxes Creek was an affluent of the
Schoharie and the "place" is near to Fuchs's
dorp at the junction of the two streams.
There is no record of a patent having been
issued for the described purchase, but we hear

* Sims's *Schoharie Co.*

of it again in an application to the Governor
by Philip Schuyler,* "for himself and the rest
of the heirs of Dr. Staats," for a license to
purchase lands at Schoharie. This application
was made in 1716. In the next year a survey
was ordered for Rip van Dam and Philip
Schuyler "for himself." What became of
"the rest of the heirs" does not appear. Nor
does it appear that these two men ever came
into possession of Schoharie lands. The
items are noted as suggestive of the kind of
discipline the Palatines were being subjected to.

A more notable suggestion is found in a record that in 1716, Feb. 10, John Christ Gerlach
petitioned for license to purchase 150 acres of
vacant and unappropriated lands at Schoharie.
This Gerlach was probably of the family of
the head man of Garloch's drop. No action
was taken on this petition, and no license
granted. It begins to be evident that with
the Governor's good-will no Palatine should
secure a title in Schoharie.

Schuyler writes that there was also a patent
for land in Schoharie valley issued to Governor Hunter and called Huntersfield. This

* Schuyler's *Col. N. Y.*, ii., 433.

does not appear among the "Land Papers," but the name Huntersfield obtained for a portion of the valley between the present villages of Middleburgh and Schoharie, and was in frequent use until within the memory of men now living. How the name could originate without such patent, or whether the name, arising in some other way, gave currency to the statement that the patent existed, are questions that need not detain us.

Not until more than five years after Hunter's return to England does it appear that any Palatine obtained title to land in the valley, save by purchase from the five partners. Then, in 1725, "William York and Lewis York, Palatines," obtained a warrant of survey for 600 acres, south of the Vroman and Schuyler patents. Possibly an exception to this statement exists in the record that Godfreid De Wolven, undoubtedly a Palatine, in May, 1722, petitioned for a grant of "150 acres of the land lying vacant and unappropriated in this province." Within sixty days he received both a warrant of survey and a certificate for "150 acres in the County of Albany." This entry does not show that De

Wolven's land was at Schoharie, tho there is nothing to indicate to the contrary, the valley of Schoharie being at that time part of Albany County.

One other land patent remains to be noted. This, after several petitions and warrants, was finally granted to Lewis Morris, Jr., and Andries Coeymans. These men, from New York, discovered that the lands along Fox Creek were not included in the patent of the five partners, and at once applied for them. The land was the same as that applied for, but not obtained by Van Dam and Philip Schuyler. For some reason, Morris and Coeymans were more successful. They secured the title in 1726, and at once made common cause with the five "Gentlemen of Albany." The two companies together were thereafter spoken of as the "Seven Partners." We should note, however, that this union of the companies did not occur until the dispute with the Palatines was practically over. A large portion of that people had already retired from the valley, while those who remained had settled their minds to make the best of the situation without further contention.

A curious item in the Land Papers is a "List of names to be inserted in the Patent for Lawyer's purchase at Schoharie, containing by estimation about 40,000 acres." This bears date of June, 1723. It is impossible to identify such purchase, tho in the next few years purchases by Lawyers—all Palatines— are noted as being allowed by the government. The estimate of acreage is absurdly exaggerated. But this, and the following records referred to, show the change of disposition towards the Palatines which had come to the gubernatorial mind after Hunter's departure.

From the grants given by Hunter, we perceive that all that portion of the valley occupied by the Palatines was so deeded away from them, that they could retain the meadows they had broken and the homes they had builded only by purchase or lease from a company of land-grabbers. There were involved in this the most unscrupulous greed, and the most inexcusable oppression recorded of colonial times. Had not Hunter's disappointment and anger so blinded him, he could never have set his hand to instruments of

such injustice. So doing was altogether unlike his better self.

The character of these transactions has
rarely been understood. The Palatines have
been represented as squatting on lands which
did not belong to them, and refusing to pay
either purchase-money or rent to the rightful
owners. This is true only by a legal fiction.
The Palatines should have been the legal
owners. The legal title was originated by
the Governor's patent, which should have
issued to the Palatines. There was no reason,
other than the Governor's will to harass that
people, for the granting said patents to the
five partners. They are also described as
"riotous, turbulent, and rebellious," when in
fact they were simply contending for the right
to live as freemen. For fifteen years from
the day of their landing on Nutten Island
they were forced to struggle for their rights
against tremendous odds. It is true that for
the first two years the government subsisted
them, but at the same time, while doling out
this "charity" with one hand, the authorities
were with the other pressing upon them with
no little severity. In the end, the people

never obtained what they regarded, and we also must regard, as their just due. Those who remained in Schoharie were compelled at last to purchase their titles from the partners, while the majority, wearying of the struggle and too high-spirited to yield to the demands of the usurpers, departed from the land which had broken its promise to their hope.

There can be little doubt as to the rise of their trouble. So large a settlement as that at the Manor must have drawn the attention of the entire colony, a regard more interested because of the peculiar relation of the government to the settlers. When the "design" broke down and this body of Palatines, at least seven hundred strong, passed up the river and through Albany, on their way to "the land of promise," curiosity was at once excited as to the quality of that valley which had exerted such magnetic power. The Palatines were the real openers of the valley and by going thither advertised it to the notice of the "Gentlemen at Albany," who early discovered both the Palatines' lack of title and the Governor's resentful temper. Thus the former

became an easy prey and the latter most sup-
ple an instrument for their greed. One read-
ing the disgraceful tale can but dwell upon the
pity of the fact that, while the Governor could
justly claim the protection and guidance of the
Queen's command in all the business of the tar,
he should so completely have forgotten her
other command, to have special concern for
"the comfort and advantage of the Palatines."
In 1718, he made a statement of the situation,
which he knew to be false, to the effect that
the people "went and took possession of Lands
granted to several persons at New York and
Albany Against repeated Orders." This was
written to the Board of Trade as an offset to
the "Statement of Grievances," which Weiser
had presented in petition to the king. Hardly
any statement could be more disingenuous.
Taken as Hunter meant it to be understood,
it justified all the afflictions of the Palatines;
while taken as the succession of events required, it condemned every action against
them.* In the same letter the Governor says:

"In compassion to the Innocent Women and children
I prevailed with the proprietors of these lands to make

* *Doc. Hist.*, iii., 422 ; *Col. Hist.*, v., 509.

them an offer of the Lands, free from all rent or acknowledgment for ten years, and ever after at a very
moderate Quit Rent. The Majority accepted the conditions, but durst not, or could not, execute the agreement for fear of the rest."

The Governor then proposes to move the
people again, and settle them " on a great
tract of land, very remote on the Frontiers,
formerly granted to Dominie Dellius, of fifty
miles square, and resumed by Act of Assembly."
Of this proposed removal we shall hear again.

Meanwhile the " Five Partners " proceeded
to assert their rights to the lands which the
Palatines had occupied. They informed the
poor people, that they had obtained the land
from the Governor, and that all living upon it
must either buy or lease their holdings, and
that such as were unwilling to do either must
leave the valley altogether. The reply of the
Palatines was that the lands of Schoharie had
been set apart for them by Queen Anne, and
that now it was the King's, and they could not
" agree with any body about the King's land."
This was sufficiently explicit, but not satisfac-
tory to the " Gentlemen of Albany," who
promptly made their appeal to the courts.

However inequitable or unjust their claim, yet their legal title was clearly defined, and the court could do no otherwise than to enforce it. In consequence of the orders of court, Sheriff Adams of Albany County, presently appeared in Schoharie, provided with appropriate legal documents, to summons the recusant settlers, to "affix papers on the land," and to arrest the more turbulent of the people. Among his papers was a special warrant, addressed to the Justices of the Counties of Albany and Dutchess, for the arrest of "John Conrade Wiser," who is described as "a Covenanted Servant of his Majesty, who has been Guilty of Several Mutinous, Riotous, and other disobedient and illegal practices, now skulking in your County to avoid punishment."

It was unfortunate for the sheriff that he had not provided himself with a *posse* as well as with papers, for the people showed no respect for his papers, and in the absence of defenders wrought a very rough will upon him.

The chief culprit, Weiser, had disappeared, but Adams undertook the arrest of the others. The first attempt, made at Weiser's dorp, brought on a riot in which the women took

vigorous and leading part.   Led by Magdalena
Zeh, the women attacked the sheriff, knocked
him down and beat him ; then they dragged
him through the nastiest puddles of their barn-
yards, and, putting him on a rail, "rode him
skimington" through the settlements, a distance of seven miles or more, and finally left
him, with two broken ribs, on a bridge well
out on the road to Albany.   So tradition, as
recorded by Sims, enters into detail.   Very
likely the story is exaggerated, tho so far
as the female actors are concerned it may easily
find belief.   The Palatine women were stal-
wart as the famous "women of Marblehead."
It was no uncommon thing for them, while as
yet for two or three years no mill was built
at Schoharie, to carry on their backs their corn
to the mill at Schenectady, going thither and
returning in one day.

When the sheriff returned to Albany and
reported to the partners, they were at a loss
for further proceedings which might be effective.   For a while they pursued a policy of
silence and left the people unmolested, refrain-
ing from further coercive measures until the
Governor should come to Albany.   This visit
16

of Hunter was made in 1717, for the double purpose of holding a conference with the Indians and settling this business of the Palatines. He sent orders to Schoharie for a deputation of three men from each village to meet him at Albany, and particularly that Captain Weiser should be of the deputation. Inasmuch as the Governor had publicly said that he would hang Weiser, if he got hold of him, very naturally the captain did not present himself with the deputies. The others appeared before the Governor and were sharply rated for their refractory conduct. There is a series of three questions and answers very succinctly put in the Palatine Statement, which shows that in the encounter of wits they got the better of the Governor.

He asked the deputies:

1. Why they went to Schoharie without his orders?

2. Why they did not agree with the Gentlemen of Albany? and

3. Why they concerned themselves so much with the Indians?

To these the deputies replied:

1. The Governor had told them to shift for

themselves, and they were compelled to go somewhere and do something.

2. The demands of the Albany Gentlemen were extravagant—while the Palatines had received the lands from the King. If they served anybody, it must be the King, and not private persons.

3. It was necessary for them on that exposed frontier, to be in good terms with the Indians as a protection against the French and hostile Indians.

Clearly the deputies had the best of the argument, but this availed nothing with the Governor, who finished the hearing by sharply commanding them to either agree with the Albany Gentlemen or leave the valley, and forbidding them to plow and sow the ground until the necessary agreement with the five partners had been made. With this the deputies returned to Schoharie and Hunter to New York. In the following winter—no agreement with the partners having been made—the people sent three men to New York to ask permission from the Governor to plow the lands in the coming spring. The "Statement" represents the Governor as replying to this request, in a Pilate-like brevity, "What is said, is said." Then in its amusingly pathetic grandiose style, the account goes on :

"This was a thunder-clap in the ears of their Wifes and children and the lamentation of all the people increased to such a hight, and their necessity grew so great, that they were forced for their own preservation to transgress those orders, and sow some summer corn and fruits or else they must have starved."

There is in a letter of Sec'y Clarke to Mr. Walpole, written in November of 1722,* an almost open confession that in these and previous proceedings the Palatines had been treated with injustice. He refers to a form of certificate sent by Hunter, after his return to England, for the signatures of the Palatines. It will be remembered that one reason of Hunter's return home was that he might prosecute his claim for reimbursement for advances on the Palatine account. There the Lords of the Treasury demanded as vouchers, not only the receipts of Livingston for the moneys paid, but the acknowledgment of the Palatines themselves, that they had been subsisted according to contract and the Queen's orders.

* *Doc. Hist.*, iii., 429.

But such certificate they were, as the Secretary says, "most unwilling to sign, fearing new snares and contracts." He notes that a great many of them had already purchased land in Pennsylvania and were determined to go thither; and concludes, "Thus the Brigadeer is baulked, and this province deprived of a good frontier of hardy and Laborious people. His claim is Just, his request reasonable, but that threatening manner of proceeding has injured him beyond expression." There can be no doubt that, had Hunter pursued a just course towards the Palatines, they would not have denied him the certificate demanded, and himself would have come nearer to just treatment by the Treasury.

In the spring of 1718, when the people found themselves "forced to sow some summer corn and fruits," they came to the conclusion that neither kindness nor justice was to be expected from the Governor or the Gentlemen of Albany, and that appeal must be made to a higher power. To this end they appointed three of their best men to go to London and lay their grievances before the King. Their statement, from which copious quotations have already been made, was probably written by the elder Weiser. Tho amusing by its quaint turgidity and also overstrained by the bias of the writer, it gives marked token of intellectual power. No ignorant hand put together that effective document, which is both logical and graphic, and allowing for the exaggeration of style, adheres much more closely to the truth than did Governor Hunter. This appeal to the justice and kindness of King George was carried to London by Weiser, Scheff, and Walrath. These two companions of Weiser find mention only in connection with this mission. Walrath died in London, before the mission was completed. Scheff, after Walrath's death, quarrelled with Weiser and returned to America in 1721, and six months after his arrival died in New York city.

The departure of the deputies from Schoharie had to be by stealth. Probably Weiser had disappeared from the valley several months before, and was joined by his companions at some place on the route to Philadelphia. From that city they set sail for England; but their ship had hardly issued from between the Capes,

when it was taken by " pirates." These seem
to have been milder-mannered men than the
average of the sea-rovers. They neither
scuttled the ship nor cut a throat, preferring
robbery without murder and wreck. They
stripped the ship of everything valuable, leaving to its crew and passengers only clothing
sufficient for their nakedness and food to subsist them until they could reach Boston. They
took the money of the Palatine deputies, and,
not regarding it as enough, triced up Weiser
and scourged him to compel a confession of a
hidden purse. This discipline was suffered
three times, when at last the pirates were in-
duced to believe Scheff's tearful protestations,
that the entire money of the company was in
the purse taken from himself. When released
by the robbers, the ship sailed to Boston and
thence, being resupplied, resumed its voyage
to England. Weiser and his companions
reached London absolutely penniless. They
sent home for such remittances as their friends
could forward, and meanwhile had to live as
best they could on kindness and credit. These
did not stead them very long, the hoped-for
supply of funds from America was delayed,

and the poor unfortunates were thrown into the debtor's prison. There they suffered great misery, in the midst of which, and by force of which, Walrath died. To this also may be attributed the death of Scheff, a few months after his liberation.

In their prison the deputies found means of reaching the ears of the authorities on the matters of their mission. Their petition was presented to the government and, apparently, was referred to the Lords of Trade for consideration and the advisement of the King. In response the Board of Trade made a comment of some length.* They recite that, under the terms of settlement, the Palatines were "to be maintained at her Majesty's expense until so settled as to provide for themselves." Then alluding to the failure of the experiment, the protesting of Hunter's bills, and the dispersion of the Palatines, they state that "they settled themselves in a riotous manner on lands belonging to other persons." Thus the false representations of Hunter had found credence—and most naturally—in the minds of the Lords of Trade, and were final in the non-

* *Col. Hist.*, v., 601.

suiting of the Palatines. By the time, also,
that their petition came up for hearing,
Hunter* himself was in England and, tho he
had not influence enough to secure justice for
himself, he was able to confirm the injustice of
his own treatment of the poor people, whom
"the Queen's clemency" had committed to his
care, with the strict charge that everything
should be done "with a view to the comfort of
the poor Palatines." Destitute of all friends
at court and without means to procure talents
to plead their cause, it was inevitable that the
mere statement of the poor debtors, languish-
ing in prison, should be light as air in the
scales against the assertion of so high a servant of the crown as the Governor of the province, who, we may readily believe, did not
fail to embellish his narrative with a description of the riotous and rebellious character of
the Palatines. His influence was fatal to the
petition. There is some satisfaction to the
reader's sense of poetic justice in the reflection,
that the very means with which the Governor
effected this oppression of the people, proved
the knife which cut the throat of his own

* *Col. Hist.*, v., 552.

hopes. The crisis of his own cause turned against him through the lack of their testimony.

The long-delayed remittances from America at last arriving, the surviving deputies were liberated from prison. Shortly afterwards Scheff parted from Weiser and addressed an independent petition to the Board of Trade.* He recites the same facts as the former statement, tho in less ambitious style and with some added items of interest. He says that there are "about 160 families, and about 1000 souls at Schoharie . . . they had built huts, houses, and mills, improved the ground, and had made a road about 24 miles to Albany." He further says that there were about five hundred Palatine families, or three thousand souls, in the province, and asks that "they all be settled above, below, or round about the valley of Schorie." Then he protests against the patents given for the Schoharie lands as acts of bad faith, in the following words :

" And considering that the grant of the valley of Schorie, supposed to be given to some Gentlemen of Al-

* *Col. Hist.*, v., 557.

bany, having been made some time after the said Germans
had seated themselves thereon, at first to one and afterwards to two other persons, was, as they humbly conceive,
against the Plantation Laws, for the truth of which they
humbly appeal to the proceedings of the Assembly of
the Province, and those of the Governor and Council."

Here Scheff exposes the real nature of the
wrong. He also deprecates removal from
Schoharie on account of the unavoidable ex-
posure of the women and children to the dan-
gers of another transportation. If, however,
they are to be removed, he claims that they
should receive compensation for the better-
ments made by them in the valley.

Having lodged this petition, Scheff returned
homeward, broken both in spirit and in health.
Weiser remained in London two years longer,
apparently "hoping against hope" that he
might yet in some way secure an influence, by
which relief could come for his people and himself. It was not until 1723, after five years of
sojourn in London, in the midst of great suffering, that he finally gave up the struggle and
returned to America.

Meanwhile, during his absence, the people
had remained at Schoharie. They "continued

to improve the land," they plowed and planted
and reaped, not much molested by the " Partners," who were biding their time, but conscious
that their tenure was very slight, destitute of
any rights of freehold which the law could
sustain.   For a long time after the maltreat-
ment of the sheriff they were very "shy" of
Albany.   Sims states that the men of the
valley would not go to Albany on any business,
and sent the women thither for salt and other
such necessities, themselves venturing to the
city only upon Sundays, when they supposed
that process could not be served upon them.
After some months, however, during which the
partners had made no sign, the people began
to think that the trouble had blown over and
that the violence to the sheriff was forgotten.
So thinking, a party of the men went to Albany
on a week-day, and were promptly arrested and
thrown into gaol.   The charges against them
were of riot and trespassing.   There seems
to have been no pretence of a trial, the arrest
being simply a means of coercion by the partners, to compel the settlers to acknowledge their
title.   The prisoners, among whom was young
Conrad Weiser, were kept in gaol for several

days, and finally released on the agreement of
most of them to acknowledge the title of the
Albany Gentlemen, and to take their holdings
at Schoharie, either by purchase or on lease.
This scored the first victory of the partners,
and in moral effect on the Palatines it was complete. It broke the front of opposition by
the people, and made the enforcement of the
legal claim upon the lands a hundred-fold easier.
The spirit of resistance was curbed by this
defection, and the poor people realized at last
that they must yield to the stronger.

There seems to have obtained in some minds
a disproportionate idea of the discontent and
disorder of the Palatines, which, unless they
were guilty of lawless actions not recorded, is
quite unjustified. The treatment given to
Adams stands alone in violent character. In
all the rest of the story—their enemies being
recorders—the movements of opposition were
simply the refusal of manly spirits to submit
to oppressive and unjust demands. The refusal was made the more sturdy by a consciousness of constant fraud in the action of
governmental agents towards them. Dr.
Homes comments on their "discontent," as

though it were blameworthy. But on a faithful presentation of the facts there is room for wonder, that their discontent did not receive a more frequent and more violent expression. Certainly, nothing in their conduct, other than the incident of the sheriff's experience, could justify the following language of Hunter :

"They might be usefully employed there [Schoharie], but there must be a Fort or two, as well to cover them as to keep them in order, which I know to be a hard task by dear bought experience, and this will require an augmentation of our Forces." *

Near the end of Hunter's term, on the request of the Board of Trade, a census of the Palatines was made, the Governor having applied to the two clergymen, Kockerthal and Hager, to procure the statistics. They reported in 1718—that the numbers in the Province of New York were as follows—

East side of Hudson River..126 Families : 499 Persons.
West side of the River...... 68   "   272   "
New York city............. 30   "   150   "
"Skohare "................170   "   680   "
                         ————   ————
              Total, 394   "   1601   "

* *Col. Hist.* v. 509.

The reverend census-takers state that this enumeration does not include the widows and orphans !—a somewhat curious fact, which gives room for questioning the correctness of their "list" in other particulars. We may suppose that Scheff's statement of the number as three thousand is above the truth. But this estimate given to Hunter must have been equally below it. Considering that not less than twenty-five hundred were landed on Nutten Island in 1710, unless there was an unusual and unrecorded mortality among the people, the natural increase would have made them at least hold their own in numbers. They were a prolific people, and children were plentiful in their homes. An interesting record states that within the first fortnight after reaching Schoharie, the houses of Earhart, Lawyer, and Bouck were enriched by births. Of these three names two are still well known in the valley to-day. Certainly, we cannot be far wrong when estimating the Palatine population at Schoharie as above eight hundred. Nearly seven hundred composed the immigration of 1712-13. In six years the children born and the excepted widows and orphans could hardly fail of bringing the total to the suggested number. This was a large company to be settled together "on the frontier," and the fancy can paint a glowing picture of what plenty and prosperity, what commercial growth and power might have ensued, had this people been suffered to remain unmolested together, to work out a destiny for themselves and this valley of their promise and delight.

\But that was not to be. Fully two thirds of the people went forth, making for them a third migration, to seek yet other homes. Those who remained preferred submission to further unsettlement. But this large majority could not be content to buy from the hand of the oppressor what they knew to be morally their own.

As we recall the frequent expression of their hope when they set out for America ; the constancy, like that of the needle to the pole, with which their thought regarded " the promised land of Schorie " ; and the elation with which they passed within the embrace of its glorious hills,—entering the kingdom through much tribulation,—we can understand something of the tenacity of their ten years' struggle against their foes, and something of the pang with which they turned their backs on "Schorie." Poetry and art have done their best to depict the sorrows of Acadia and its exiled people. And there was, indeed, a tragic quality to their experience, an intrusion of ruthless and brutal force, which are lacking happily from the Story of the Palatines. Thus there was a dignity in the sufferings of the poor Acadians, which also is lacking in the lot of the Palatines. And yet the latter suffered, if not so severely, certainly as wrongfully. Somehow—no one can explain it—to suffer at the bidding of military necessity adds honor to the pangs; while they, who are the helpless victims of spite and greed, seem to be smirched with the baseness of their foes, and to appeal in vain to the sympathies of history.

CHAPTER VII.

THE DISPERSION.

THE beginning of the dispersion and final migrations of these people is found in the instruction of the Board of Trade to Governor Burnett, shortly after his coming to New York. Sec'y Popple's letter, dated 29 Nov. 1720, directed the Governor to "settle those among the Palatines, who behave themselves with due submission to His Majesty's authority and are destitute of means of subsistence, upon such convenient lands as are not already disposed of." Possibly the petition of Weiser did so much of good as to convince the government that, if they could not right the wrongs of the Palatines, they must at least find them a place of unmolested habitation.

Burnett's thought,* as he wrote to London,

* *Col. Hist.*, v., 634.

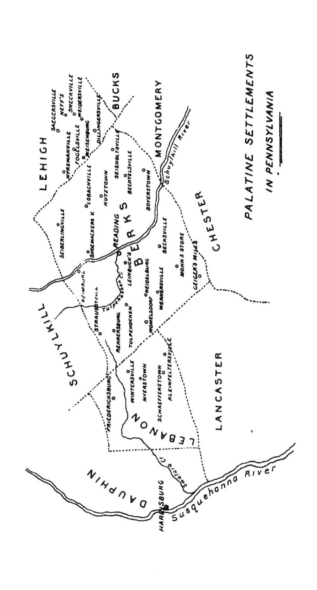

PALATINE SETTLEMENTS
IN PENNSYLVANIA

was to settle them "in the middle of our Indians. But they could not be brought to that.
. . . I have granted their request to purchase of the Mohocks." This so pleased them that "all who did live in a lawless manner on the Land of Schokerry, which had been granted to other proprietors, have now actually taken leases and *attorned* Tenants." Evidently, the Governor, in his desire to report the establishment of peace, was not conscious of the absurdity of this statement. If the recalcitrant people had all taken leases at Schoharie, the need of any purchases among the "Mohocks" could not have been very pressing. Undoubtedly, the mood of Burnett was much more amicable towards the Palatines than was that of Hunter, tho it is clear that the statements of the latter had moulded his opinions as to the character of the people and the situation. Weiser writes :

"The new Governor felt like conciliating the disaffected, but they were nevertheless obliged to see their best acres abandoned, or retained at enormous prices. Some made a virtue of necessity and fell in with the new order, even at the expense of their manhood. Others would rather scatter here and there over the Province."

The "Land Papers" show that under this
pressure the minds of many of the people were
turned towards the Mohawk valley as the only
way of escape. In the year 1722 various records were made of petitions for license to purchase land on the Mohawk, of warrants of
survey, of Indian deeds, and of drafts of
patents given to Palatines. We do not need
to particularize in detail. One grant issued
to Garlock, whose petition for Schoharie land
had failed; another to Conrad Weiser, Jun.;
and yet another to Hartman Vinedecker, one
of the chiefs from whose first name the name
of Hartman's dorp was made. Several of
these permits recite often the names of the
principals, "and other distressed Palatines,"
which may perhaps suggest some slight com-
punctions of the official conscience as to the
distresses of that people. One license permits
young Weiser to "purchase in the Mohawks
country, three miles distant from any part of
the Mohawks river,"—and this might suggest
a desire, on the Governor's part, that so trouble-
some a stock as that of Weiser might be put
off into the woods and as far as possible from
the natural channels of communication. One

of the Indian deeds is much more liberal,
ceding to the same Weiser lands stretching
" westerly 24 miles on Mohawk's River to Gan-
endagaran [Canajoharie ?], on both sides of
the river, and [north and south] as far as said
Palatin or High Dutchmen, please."

To these various warrants and licenses Burnett alludes when he writes—November 21,
1722 : " I have given them leave to purchase
land from the Indians, between the present
English settlements near Fort Hunter and
part of Canada [?], on a creek called Canada
Creek." He defines this leave as given to
" about sixty families, who desired to be in a
distinct tract from the rest, and were those
who all along had been most hearty for the
government." This latter statement is another
of Burnett's absurdities, for those who were
most submissive and hearty to the government
had contented themselves in taking leases in
Schoharie.

Burnett sees much value in planting the
Palatines on the Mohawk, as they will there ·
be " a barrier against sudden incursions of the
French, who made this their road when they
last attacked and burned the Frontier town

called Schonectady." In this letter Burnett
speaks very disparagingly of the Palatines. " I
find very little gratitude for favors done them."
Under all the circumstances this is explicable,
without reflecting severely on their character.
Evidently, the Governor was somewhat vexed.
He had gone up to Albany about this and
other business, and had expected, as he wrote
in this same letter,

" to fix the Palatines in their new settlements which I
had obtained of the Indians [!] at a very late purchase,
but I found them very much divided into Parties. They
said that the lands were not enough, the cunningest
among them fomenting their Divisions, in order that
the greatest number might leave the Province, and then
the great Tract of Land lately purchased would make
so many considerable estates to the few Families that
should remain. . . . This is managed by a few cunning
persons who lead the rest as they please, who are for the
generality a laborious and honest, but headstrong and
ignorant, people."

Burnett seems to have possessed an inventive mind ; and yet this letter is not consistent
with itself. Nor is it consistent with the fact
that "the cunningest among them," such as
Weiser and Vinedecker, did not go to that
"great Tract" at all. They tarried yet a while

in Schoharie and then themselves, not their
dupes, left the province altogether and went
into Pennsylvania.

\ The origin of that migration to Pennsylvania
has some connection with the other business
which brought Burnett to Albany in 1722.
That was attendance at one of the frequent
councils with the Indians. Albany was the
point at which the negotiations with the
friendly tribes were carried on, the scene of
many a long palaver, and the emporium of
the Indian trade. Here was the official residence of the provincial Secretary for Indian
affairs, and hither came the Governor to meet
his "Brothers" of the tribes in solemn con-
clave. The Council of this year was of more
than usual importance, because of movements
and agreements among the Indians, by which
the tribes beyond the borders of New York
were affected. This larger interest and importance of the Council drew to its delibera-
tions, not only the Governor of New York,
but also Sir William Keith, the Governor of
Pennsylvania. While at Albany Keith be- .
came acquainted with the Palatine affairs.
Probably Burnett discoursed to him of the

trouble they had given to Hunter and himself, and some of the leading Palatines told him of their afflictions and unrest. In whatever way Keith may have been informed, he was moved to compassion towards the distressed people, and offered to them an asylum from all persecution in his own province. Weiser * says that he, "hearing of the unrest of the Germans, lost no time to inform them of the freedom and justice accorded to their countrymen in Pennsylvania."

This "afforded" alludes to the kindly reception already given to immigrants from the Palatinate directly to Pennsylvania. In 1717† five years before the visit of Keith to Albany, and while the Schoharie troubles were at their height, three ship-loads of Palatines were landed at Philadelphia. The captains of the ships reported their arrival, furnished a list of their passengers, and, as though aware that such an influx was unusual for both numbers and nationality, requested from the council permission to land the people. This was at once given, while the names of the immigrants were put on record and are still preserved,

* *Life of Weiser*, p. 28.   † *Penn. Col. Records*, iii., 29.

together with the names of over thirty thousand of their countrymen from the Palatinate
and other parts of Germany, who during the
next thirty years came from the old country
directly to Pennsylvania. The peculiarity of
this record of names consists in the fact, that
such was not kept of other immigrants into
that province. We may suppose that the unusual nationality of this first company, or its
numbers (363), suggested the propriety of the
record; the continuance of which was regarded
as important, because of the volume of the
incoming during the next three decades. For
whatever reason caused, the Palatines in Pennsylvania have this distinction,—that they alone
among the early settlers of that commonwealth
have, name by name, their place in the records .
of the colony.

There can be little doubt that the change
of direction on the part of this company of
1717 from New York to Philadelphia, was due
to the report of tribulations sent home by the
Palatines of the Manor and Schoharie. The
treatment they had received, the harsh service,
and the unrelenting persistence which denied
a foothold, convinced the newcomers that

New York would not afford them hospitable welcome or happy homes. So they bethought them of the invitation sent to the oppressed in Europe, thirty years before, by William Penn, offering a welcome refuge in his new colony in America. They sailed directly to Philadelphia from Rotterdam, touching neither at any English port nor at New York. So doing, they became more successful pioneers for their countrymen than were the settlers on the Hudson and the Schoharie. After their experiences no company of Palatines came of their own accord to New York. To this there is one apparent exception.

In 1722* a single ship with a large company of people arrived at New York, having "touched in England" on the way from Holland. But its going thither may be set down as compulsory, by reason of general and severe sickness on board. The inspecting physicians reported to the Governor and Council that there was no "Contagious Distemper on Board the said Vessell," but suggested that the "quantity of Cloaths may have contracted Noisome Smells," because of the

* *Doc. Hist.*, iii., 428.

large number of the sick and "the Length of
the Voyage." So it was ordered by the Governor and Council that no person from the
ship should "come on Shoar on this Island
[N. Y.] with any Cloaths, Chests or other
furniture till the same have been thoroughly
air'd upon Nutton Island during the space of
six hours at least."

On this ship, it may be noted in passing,
were four men of the name of Erghimer, the
son of one of whom, to the glory of the New
York Palatines, was Nicholas Herkimer, the
hero of Oriskany. With this one exception
of a ship probably carried out of its intended ·
course, all the Palatine immigrations after
1710 landed at Philadelphia. And it is well ·
to note that, so large was the Palatine element
in these immigrations, all the natives of other
German States, coming with them, were called
by the same name. Thus, though the Palatinate covered but a small portion of the
German Empire, yet for forty years in Pennsylvania nomenclature all Germans were Palatines.

It should be noted here that, previous to the
migration from Schoharie and the consequent

large influx directly from the old country, several companies of Germans had come to Pennsylvania. Most of them were small bands of religionists, whose peculiar views made life a burden to them in the fatherland. So early as 1685 a band of Mennonites settled at Germantown, giving the spot its name. About the same time Labadists from Frieseland settled in Newcastle County, Delaware, then a part of Pennsylvania. Ten years after, Kelpius brought a company of Pietists and settled them on the Wissahickon ; and in 1719 a band of Dunkers settled in Germantown by the side of the Mennonites. Other religious sects were added in the next few years,—the Newborn, the Disciples of Ephrata, and the Schwenkfelders, closing the list with the large and beneficent incoming of the Moravians, which began in 1735.* About 1705 or 1712, came to Philadelphia that distinct company of Germans, who passed over into New Jersey, having New York as their objective, but were so charmed by the rolling lands of Morris County that they quietly took possession.†

* Mellick's *Story of an Old Farm* ; Sachse's *German Pietists of Pennsylvania* ; Rupp's *Collection*.   † See page 60.

It is probable that this last-mentioned company were Palatines. If in 1712, they may have landed at Philadelphia instead of New York by stress of storm, having in mind to join their countrymen on the Hudson, of whose hard fortunes they had not yet heard. It is not unlikely that the tidings of those afflictions, met on their journey overland, made them all the more ready to yield to the attractions of the Jersey hills. But, except for this and the immigration of 1717 already noted, it is impossible to connect any of these other companies with the Palatines. They came from other parts of Germany and from diverse motives. At the same time it is clear that the immense tide of German immigration, which after 1720 set into Pennsylvania, was dominantly Palatine, and was controlled as to its destination by the kindly treatment received by its forerunners at the hands of the Quakers.

Governor Keith could truthfully tell the men of Schoharie that their countrymen had been "afforded freedom and justice" in his province. The bands of religionists had been in no way molested. The immigrants of 1717 also had been received with the utmost kind-

ness, and the people had been allowed to choose
their places of residence.   The most of them
settled about sixty miles west of Philadelphia,
and were subjected to no other trials than
those incident to a new settlement in the forest
in the vicinage of capricious Indians.   This
invitation of Keith found open ears with many
of the Palatines at Schoharie, whose formal
petition to Governor Keith and the Assembly
of Pennsylvania was soon forwarded to Philadelphia.*   The petition was from fifteen (heads
of family ?) at Schoharie, who recited in brief
their experiences since leaving Europe, stated
that they had heard of the generous treatment
shown to their countrymen in Pennsylvania,
and prayed that lands might be set aside for
them on the Tulpehocken, which lands they
declared themselves ready and able to purchase.   This petition was not immediately
acted on by the Assembly, but it appears † from
a similar petition presented three years after-
ward, and after the first company from Schoharie had already come into Pennsylvania, that
the immigration thither was with the full consent of the authorities.   The fact that the

* Rupp's *Berks Co., Pa.*, p. 98.   † *Penn. Col. Records.*, iii., 322.

presence of the people was on invitation of
Keith is noted by the Assembly, and steps are
taken towards satisfying the claims of Chief
Sassouan, who had protested against the occupancy of the Tulpehocken lands.

These various statements show that in 1723
the settlers at Schoharie were divided in three
parts. The one resolved to remain in the valley at the cost of whatever "agreement" they
could make with the usurpers of their lands.
The others could not bring themselves to submit to such humiliating conditions, and "girded
up their loins" for a third removal—one part
of them to the Mohawk, and the rest into
Pennsylvania. Of the numbers in these several
sections of the people it is impossible to speak
with any exactness.

Probably about three hundred remained in
Schoharie. Their life there was uneventful,
so far as any incident is presented for record
here. For the most part, having made terms
with the patentees, they were suffered to live
out their lives in peace. Occasionally roving
bands of Indians extended their depredating
tours into the valley, but, happily for the settlers, its secluded situation, southward from the

great Indian thoroughfare along the Mohawk
and sheltered among the mountains, saved
them from the refluent tide of war, which so
often for thirty years made the Mohawk and
the northern country a bloody ground. In the
Revolution, Brandt with his Indians and English allies went down the valley. He made a
sharp attack on the fort at Middleburgh, and
was beaten off, and left as memento of his
raid a cannon ball in the freize of the old Stone
Church at Fox's dorp, which still can be seen
by the visitor of historic taste, held fast in the
spot where Brandt placed it. Much romance
finds its home in the valley, and many tales of
adventure are related of Murphy, the Indian
fighter, whom Brown styles the "Benefactor
of Schoharie." The Schoharie people were a
quiet folk, content to farm their lands and ed-
ucate their children, and have left no special
marks upon the history of the State, save in the
person and life of William C. Bouck, a man
of very considerable ability, of direct Palatine
descent, who held various public offices of
trust and honor from the State, and served
with dignity as its governor from 1843–45.
There was in vogue, some forty years ago, the

bye-word, "Ignorant as a Schoharie Dutch-
man." How this slighting comparison originated it is hard to tell, but there is no doubt
of its injustice, for it can be successfully maintained that, for general intelligence, sobriety,
probity, and industry the villages on the Schoharie were not a whit behind the average rural
community of New York State.

We turn now to the Mohawk, whither migrated at least a third of the Palatines of Schoharie, to whose number were added many from
the solitary ship which arrived in New York
in 1722, among them the families of Erghimer.
The leader of the men from Schoharie was
Elias Garloch, one of the seven chiefs or deputies, who came as prospectors from the Manor.
He was the head of Garloch's dorp in the valley, and, as already noted, had unsuccessfully
applied for a patent in Schoharie. While in
Schoharie he occupied the position of magistrate, either by appointment from Albany or
by choice of his countrymen. One of the
many whose sense of right and manhood would
not permit them to make any composition with
the unjust patentees, he resolved to give up the
long-cherished hope which had made Schoharie

18

as a land of promise, to abandon the home he had built and the improvements made through twelve years' labor in the valley, and set out again to find still another settlement.

Of course, Garloch was not singular in this feeling and resolution.   At least two thirds of the eight hundred people in Schoharie were in perfect sympathy and agreed with him therein. This fact is notable.   And this is not to be explained by any supposition of an unreasonable and unruly spirit.   Such explanation would be reasonable for the wayward conduct of a mere handful of men.   But it will not do for two thirds of a community, to the number of five hundred and more.   For eight years the question had been mooted, the patentees had asserted their claim, and offered easy terms of settlement, so that some among the Palatines were seduced into compliance.   But to these terms this great majority had returned only a stubborn negative,   They refused to either lease or buy the lands which, in all justice, were their own.   The lands were cheap enough.   They could secure titles to them at less cost than the expense of removing elsewhere, but in no way would they admit the claim of the patentees. When after these years of quiet struggle, in which occurred but one outbreak, they found that permanent settlement in Schoharie was only possible at the loss of self-respect, they set out for other dwelling-places. It was not done "in a pet," nor in disorder, but in the quietness of determined resistance to wrong. Such is the only proper understanding of their course. Some have flippantly spoken of it as ignorant and stubborn. Ignorant these people certainly were not, but had clear view both of right and truth. As to stubbornness, theirs was of the same sort as that which emptied the tea chests into the waters of Boston harbor.

We have already noted the fact that warrants of survey and for patents of land in the "Mohawks country" had been issued to Garloch, Winedecker, Weiser, and others before 1723. Of these three only the first entered upon the land so granted, the attention of Winedecker and Weiser having been turned towards Pennsylvaina. In the latter part of 1725 a patent was issued for lands on the Mohawk, "twenty-four miles westerly from Little Falls, on both sides of the river," to

William Burnett and others. This Burnett
was undoubtedly the Governor and the
"others" were Palatines, ninety-two of whom
are named in the instrument. We understand
that these ninety-two were mainly heads of
families, so that this migration must have included over three hundred persons. The
patent is called the Burnetsfield patent, from
the name of the Governor, the inclusion of
which in the instrument was for some purpose
not mentioned. Certainly, he made no claim
of personal title to these lands, to the distress
of the Palatines, after the manner of the five
partners in Schoharie. His purpose in associat-
ing himself with the Palatines in this patent
was, probably, with a view of facilitating the
partition of the lands among the settlers.
The patent recites that "one hundred acres
were to be given to each person, man, woman,
and child." This amount was a free grant,
subject only to the usual quit-rent to the crown.
In addition to this, others, like Garloch and
Eckaard, had independent patents and were
able to purchase lands beyond.

To this region the people removed in 1725–
'26, and made new homes which, happily, were

to be permanent, and gave to various localities the names which to-day testify of their possession. For twenty-five or thirty miles the Mohawk is to-day a Palatine, or German, river. A glance at the map will show how true this is, with its names of towns which this people knew in the fatherland, monuments of their early possession and settlement. Thus the two towns of Palatine and Palatine Bridge show clearly the source of their names. Mannheim, Oppenheim, Newkirk, and others are as clearly marked with a German origin. The level meadows, unsurpassed for fertility, stretching along the south side of the Mohawk, are still known as the German Flats, while over against them on the north side was the settlement, which in after-years received the name of Herkimer, from the bluff General, the most celebrated among the Palatines of the Mohawk. And not only on the river, but for long distances on either side remain like tokens of this permanent German possession.

For thirty years the people had undisputed occupancy and were unmolested, so that they enjoyed a long period of rest and peace and prosperity, after the toils and afflictions experienced in the old country and, as well also, for fifteen years in the new.* "The people were seated on as fertile a spot as any in the State. They had good buildings on their farms and were generally rich." Upon all this prosperity, however, came that ruin which visited and destroyed so many of the frontier towns during the French and Indian War. In November, 1757, occurred the raid of M. de Belletre, whose force, composed of 300 Indians and Canadians, came up the Black River valley, and emerging from the mountain forests, fell without warning on all the Palatine settlements on the north side of the Mohawk. They made a clean sweep, burning every building—alike the houses of the people and the barns stuffed with the gathered crops, while most of the stock, horses, cattle, sheep, and swine were killed. Some of the people were slain and nearly one hundred carried off as prisoners. The majority of the people saved themselves by flight, crossing the river and seeking refuge in the fort on the south side. The enemy did not pursue, but busying themselves with the work of destruction, retired

* Benton's *Herkimer Co.*, p. 58.

at nightfall with their booty and their prisoners, satisfied for that occasion.

But this satisfaction lasted only until the following spring. In April of 1758, another band of marauders, composed of a small number of French and a much larger body of Indians, attacked the settlements on the south side of the river. This party did not succeed in approaching the settlements with entire surprise. Warning was in some way given, and Captain Herchamer *—the future General—who was in command of the fort, was able to collect behind its defences the great majority of the settlers. The attack on the fort failed, but the invading force killed thirty of the Palatines and rivalled, in the destruction of the unprotected farmsteads, their comrades' work of the preceding autumn.

In the following year the fall of Quebec, and the coincident collapse of the French power in America, brought peace to the much-suffering frontiers. The Palatines were able to rebuild their houses and barns. The captives returned, and prosperity came back again

* Note the evolution of the name: Erghimer, Herchamer, Herkimer.

to stay.   In all this period this people were
notable for their bravery and devotion.   From
the settlements stretching from the Flats to
Palatine a sturdy body of yeomanry was organized in nine companies by Sir William
Johnson, who counted much upon them for
his measures of defence during the French
War.   In the after-struggles of the colonies
with England, they were very patriotic, and
resolutely refused to be drawn away by Guy
Johnson to the cause of the King.   They were
described as "very hearty in the present struggles for American liberty."   In all the dis-
tricts of Tryon County committees of Public
Safety were appointed, and among them, says
Benton, the committees of Palatine and Canajoharie seem to have taken the initiative and
the lead.   Guy Johnson, recognizing the
strength to the royal cause which would come
by winning over these people, did his utmost
to secure their defection from the popular
cause.   To all his appeals and arguments the
Palatines were deaf, and in a formal letter,
delivered by Nicholas Herkimer and Edward
Wahl,* "announced their resolution of stand-

* Benton's *Herkimer Co.*, p. 68.

ing by the country until all grievances were redressed." On receipt of this letter Johnson perceived that all present occupation for him in the Mohawk valley was gone, and retired to Canada. Thence in 1777, he came with St. Leger, only to turn back again after the baffling victory of the Oriskany. How bravely and stanchly the Palatines maintained their resolution that battle shows. To them and to their brave Herkimer, whose life was there forfeit to his glory, belongs large credit of. making possible the supreme victory of Saratoga, by which was ended the struggle for the Hudson, and the vital union of the northern colonies secured.

It only remains to narrate the fortunes of the migration to Pennsylvania. The MSS. of the younger Weiser state that "the people got news of lands on the Swatara and Tulpehocken." In what way such news reached them he does not tell, but it is not at all improbable that the locality was suggested as appropriate by the hospitable Keith. Certainly, the tidings proved attractive, and together with the Governor's invitation opened a way of escape from the toils of Schoharie. To

many of them it was far more desirable than
any new location within the province of New
York. The experiences of the people in New
York and the disposition of the authorities
towards them were of such a character, that at
least a third of the Schoharie population readily embraced the first opportunity of establishment beyond the jurisdiction of the colony in
which they had found such troubles. This we
may take as accounting for the sudden change
of plan on the part of Vinedecker and Weiser,
both of whom had obtained licences for land
on the Mohawk and were preparing to remove
thither. On the opening of this new prospect
into the colony of Pennsylvania, they either
abandoned or transferred to others their rights
under these licences, and began to arrange for
a departure to the southward. About sixty
families, or about three hundred persons, went
from Schoharie to the Tulpehocken region.
This migration, however, was not in one body,
the first detachment starting in the spring of
1723, not more than eight months after the invitation by Governor Keith, and the rest in
1728.

The leader of the first company was Hart-

man Vinedecker, the head of Hartman's dorp,
whom almost his entire village followed into
Pennsylvania.   The emigrants ascended the
Schoharie for a few miles, and then under the
conduct of an Indian guide crossed the mountains southwestwardly to the upper waters of
the Susquehanna.   On the bank of this river
they constructed canoes for the carriage of the
most of their number, with the women and
children and furniture.   In these canoes, while
some of the men drove the horses and cattle
on the land, the majority of the party floated
down the Susquehanna so far as to the mouth
of the Swatara.   Turning into this stream they
followed its upward course, until in the region
of hills and vales and fertile meadow-lands, in
which both the Swatara and Tulpehocken have
their rise, they found at last the object of their
journey and a place of permanent habitation.
To their first settlement they gave the name
of Heidelberg, and thence sent back word to
their friends at Schoharie of the prosperous
issue of the journey.   Sims has a curious tale
—gathered from some unknown source, and
hardly capable of proof or credence—that,
some months afterwards, twelve of the horses

of this company found their own way back to
the Schoharie valley. The memory of the
sweet clover on the "clawver wy"—the flats
on the Little Schoharie kill—proved superior
to all the attractions of the Tulpehocken
meadows!

The other, and probably the far smaller,
portion of the Pennsylvania migration tarried
yet five years in Schoharie, as tho with linger-
ing hope that some happy chance might yet
save them from the necessity of removal from
the beloved valley. Not until the spring of
1728 did they finally decide to join their countrymen in the south. No account is left of
the route or method of their journey, but it is
probable that they followed the course already
described by the former company. Their
leader and chief was Conrad Weiser, of whom
some things should be written, as of a character and influence worthy of very high regard.

We have noted that he was twelve years old
at the time of the emigration of his people from
the Palatinate, having had his birth at Herrenberg on November 2, 1696. He was kept at
school through boyhood until the departure of
the family to England, and in after-life he

gave abundant proof of a well-disciplined and
thoughtful mind. There are, indeed, many
writings from the hands of the two Weisers
which furnish evidence of a high degree of
intellectual and moral culture, and, for themselves at least, rebut the imputation of ignorance cast at all this people. In the first
months of the settlement at Schoharie, a friendship was formed by the Weisers with an Indian
chief of the Mohawks, named Quagnant, who
conceived a special liking for Conrad, then sixteen years of age, and proposed to take the
lad into his own country and teach him the
Indian language. The father consented, and
young Conrad himself, seeing a prospect of
adventure, was nothing loathe. He spent a
large part of the winter and following spring
in the lodge of Quagnant, and made such progress in his study of the Indian language that,
at once on his return, his services as interpreter were in demand. This service found frequent demands, not only at Schoharie, but in
Pennsylvania in his later years. He endured
great hardships among the Indians, not from
any hostility—tho several times in danger
of death by the hand of drunken braves—but

from the manner of life he was compelled to
lead. The food was unwholesome and scanty,
and his clothing was insufficient ; but the lad
showed no little grit in remaining until he had
completed his linguistic task.* From this sojourn Conrad retained a constant friendship
for the Indians, and at various times made protracted visits among them. It is supposed that
much of the time between the departures of
the first and second companies to Pennsylvania
was so spent by him, as his known position
and influence had made him specially obnoxious
to the five partners.

Out of this intimacy with the Indians came
the tale that the wife of Conrad was an Indian, to which tale the fact that the woman's
patronymic is not recorded gives color. Conrad wrote, "In 1720, while my father was
in England, I married my Anna Eve, and
was given in marriage by the Rev. John Fr.
Hager, a Reformed clergyman, on the 23d
of November, in my father's house at Schoharie." In the families of Weiser and Muhlenberg there has been no little dispute as
to the Indian origin of this Anna Eve. The

* Rupp's *Berks Co.*, p. 195 ; *Life of Weiser.*

arguments in favor are found in the Indian friendship and sojourns of young Weiser, the absence of a surname, and the fact that the marriage took place at the home of the groom, as tho the bride had no Christian home of her own from which to go to her husband. These are foundation enough for a legend, but furnish little by way of proof, and are fully met by the supposition that the young woman may have been a Redemptioner, bound out to service until the amount of her passage-money had been paid. Among the Germans coming to this country, during the early years of the last century, there were very many so indent-ured, whose surnames were lost, and after-wards had no other home or surname than those of their masters. As to Conrad's wife, her son-in-law, Muhlenberg, in the Hallische Nachrichten, declares that she was " a German Christian maiden of Evangelical parentage." This would seem to be with sufficient authority, and to justify the language of Weiser's biog-rapher : " We hesitate not to write her a full-blooded Palatine woman."

After Weiser's removal to Pennsylvania and settlement at Womelsdorf, to which place

he gave beginning and name, he soon acquired
position and influence. He was recognized
as the chief person in the German settlements,
and was frequently employed on important
missions by the Governor and Council, especially upon those in which his knowledge of
the Indian tongue made him useful. He has
left several very interesting treatises on the
Indian character, in which his special inquiry
is as to the openness of the mind of the red
men to the approach of religious teaching.
There was evidently much of a missionary
spirit in the man, and he is described as of
"unbounded benevolence, a man of integrity,
and universally respected." In many ways,
not only his own community, but the provincial
authorities relied greatly on his knowledge,
judgment, and efficiency in all affairs committed
to him. He was associated with Franklin and
other men of importance in various matters of
public concernment. Shortly after his settlement in Pennsylvania the Governor gave him
a commission as colonel; and both in the frequent Indian difficulties and through the dis-
turbances of the French War he proved the
worthiness of his rank. The only recorded

act of Weiser, which seems to reflect discredit, is his signing the petition for the disarming of the Roman Catholics, at the time of the French War. The aspect of this petition was, of course, quite contrary to the spirit of Penn, and also to the usual feelings of Weiser himself. The intent of it—and this needs to be noted—was not for religious ends, but for the protection of the colony. There were many Roman Catholics in the province, about whom public rumor busied itself with the suspicion that they would ally themselves, with their fellow-religionists from Canada, against the peace of the colony and the rights of King George. The suspicion was utterly baseless, and may be reckoned as one of those unreasonable " scares," which are apt to take possession of the mind in times of public excitement. For the moment this suspicion obtained wide credence ; and a bill in accord with the petition was passed by the Assembly. The law, however, was not generally executed, the second thought of the government having discerned its needlessness.

Weiser was of positive religious convictions and, save for a short period, a staunch

19

Lutheran. His friend and pastor, John Peter
Miller, a native of the Palatinate and graduate
of Heidelberg, led Weiser with himself into
the Seventh Day Baptist Association at
Ephrata. Miller remained in that communion until his death in 1796, but Weiser soon
retired. His house became the home of
Henry Melchior Muhlenberg, the "Patriarch
of Lutheranism" in America, from the time
that that apostle came to this country in 1742.

Not long thereafter—and this is part of
the story of the Palatines no less than of
the sketch of Weiser — Muhlenberg married
Weiser's daughter and became the father
of a celebrated progeny. No less than three
of his sons were alike clergymen, soldiers,
and statesmen, serving with distinction in pulpit, army, Congress, and other civil offices.
Frederick was Speaker of the first national
House of Representatives. One brother was
a foreign minister. Another was distinguished as a writer and scientist. Of the
eldest, Peter, it is told that he was, at the outbreak of the Revolution, a pastor in Virginia,
and took leave of his church in most dramatic
fashion. Urged by Washington, who was a

personal friend, to accept a commission as colonel in the Continental army, he consented and at once preached his farewell to his people. He told them that there was a time for everything—" a time to preach and a time to pray; but there is also a time to fight, and that time has now come." So saying, he threw off his gown and stood full dressed in his colonel's uniform. Going down from the pulpit and out of the church, he bade the drums to be beat for recruits, when more than three hundred of his congregation enlisted on the spot.

A great grandson of the Patriarch Muhlenberg was the sainted William A. Muhlenberg, so long known, venerated, and loved in New York, and whose name has to-day so sweet a fragrance in the entire American Church. There have been few families in American annals that have been more illustrious than that of the Muhlenbergs. The founder of it, tho dead over a hundred years, is still spoken of as " Father Muhlenberg" throughout Pennsylvania. Many of his descendants have laid their country under debts of gratitude and reverence; and it will be borne in mind, as one reason of their mention here, that in those descendants the blood of Weiser had equal share with that of him whose name they bore. And, indeed, without this Weiser infusion, the Muhlenbergs would, of themselves, come within the claims made on our respect and gratitude by the German and Palatine contingents to our American society and state.

Of the elder Weiser, John Conrad, but little mention is made after his return from England in 1723. His place as leader had during his absence been taken by his son, who tells in his private journal of a mission to New York:

"I was sent," he writes, "in the early part of 1721 to New York, to Gov. Burnett to hand him a petition. He received me kindly, and informed me that he had received instructions from the Lords of Trade, which he had resolved to follow implicitly."

This petition doubtless had reference to the Palatine claim to Schoharie, and the instruction must have been that, already alluded to, to settle the Palatines "on such convenient lands as are not already disposed of." John Conrad on his return to Schoharie seems to have been

quite willing to yield all leadership to the
more active Conrad. It is not at all improbable that he came back broken in health and
spirit. Certainly, he was hampered in domestic life. While yet upon the Manor he had
married again, and most unfortunately for his
own peace and his children's welfare. To them
the woman was cruel, and to him an irritation,
destroying both contentment and usefulness.
It is probable that he went with his son to
Pennsylvania, where, however, he did not remain. The details of his after-life and the
time and place of his death are not recorded.
As for the son, Conrad ; after twenty years of
useful and beneficent service in Pennsylvania,
he died at Womelsdorf in 1760.

The number of families going from Schoharie to Pennsylvania was about sixty. These
established themselves in the region of the
Tulpehocken and Swatara. There they founded a community, which from the first was
prosperous, and soon exerted a magnetic
power to draw thither thousands of their countrymen from over the sea. The treatment
received from the authorities was kindly and
generous. Shortly after their settlement, the

chief, Sassouan, complained to the Council at
Philadelphia of their intrusion on the Tulpehocken lands. He was grown old, he said,
and had never been paid for the lands, and his
children now had no place to live in. His
claim was satisfied and the Germans confirmed
in possession of the lands. To these lands,
which afterwards were delimited as Lebanon
and Berks counties, came a large proportion of
the German immigration, which at once began
to flow in with so great a volume. The map
of these counties, as that of the Mohawk,
shows in the names of its towns, many of which
names were brought from the Palatinate, how
almost exclusively this Palatine and German
element has peopled that country.

As already noted, the influx from the old
country had begun before the company had
gone from Schoharie. The movement was
accelerated and increased by the reports sent
back to Europe of the kind treatment accorded
by the Pennsylvania authorities to the immigration of 1717 and to the colony from.
Schoharie. The poor and oppressed of the
Palatinate and neighboring States realized that
at last a secure asylum was opened. Into it

they flocked in a steady stream.   Within
twenty years of the settlement at Tulpehocken
their number in the province had increased to
nearly fifty thousand, of whom a list of over
thirty thousand names is preserved in the
State archives at Harrisburg.   Very many of
them were poor and unable to pay for their
passage, and on arrival at Philadelphia were
put up at public auction to serve for a term of
years, and thus became "Redemptioners."
"They were usually sold at £10 for from .
three to five years' servitude. Many, after
serving their time faithfully, became some of
the most wealthy and influential citizens of the
state."

The unanimity with which these thousands
avoided New York is remarkable, and is com-
mented on in an interesting way by Peter
Kalm, the Swedish traveller and naturalist.
Speaking of the colony from Schoharie, he
goes on to say :

"Not satisfied with being themselves removed from
New York, they wrote to their friends and relatives, if
ever they intended to come to America, not to go to New
York. This advice had such influence that the Ger-

* Rupp's *Berks Co.*, p. 92.

mans, who afterwards went in such numbers to America, constantly avoided New York and went to Pennsylvania. It sometimes happened that they were forced to take ships bound for New York, but they were scarce got on shore when they hastened to Pennsylvania, *in sight of all the inhabitants of New York.*" *

The enormous—for those days—influx of these people into Pennsylvania occasioned at times no small alarm in the minds of some of the authorities and English inhabitants of the province. James Logan, the Secretary of the Province, wrote in 1717, when the immigration had just begun, "We have of late great numbers of Palatines poured in among us, without recommendation or notice, which gives the country some uneasiness, for foreigners do not so well among us as our own English people." †
The alarm did not spread to Jonathan Dickinson, who, some years later, wrote: "We are daily expecting ships from London, which bring over Palatines, in number about six or seven thousand. We had a parcel who came out about five years ago, and proved quiet and industrious." These six thousand must be the immigration to which Logan refers in another

---

* *Penn. Hist. Mag.*, x., 388. † Rupp's *Berks Co.*, p. 92.

letter, in which he expresses a "fear lest the colony be lost to the crown" by reason of these foreigners.

The desire for emigration seemed to be entirely appeased in the Palatinate from 1717 to 1726. Then, and probably on account of letters from Tulpehocken, it assumed new and steadier force, which was increased by the imposition of heavier burdens by the Elector. For twenty years and more there was a steady outflow, and the ships, which brought the people to America, "plied between Rotterdam and Philadelphia with almost the regularity of a ferry." In consequence of this large and continuous incoming of foreigners the authorities of the province felt called upon to take action such as no other immigration had compelled. The arrival of each ship, the numbers and names of the Palatines on board, were reported to the Council and put upon record. A special form of oath was devised for subscription by the newcomers, which recited, among other words :

"We Subscribers, Natives and late Inhabitants of the Palatinate upon the Rhine & Places adjacent . . . will be faithful and bear true allegiance to his present MA-

JESTY KING GEORGE THE SECOND, and his Successors, Kings of Great Britain, and will be faithful to the Proprietor of this Province : and will demean ourselves peaceably . . . and strictly observe and conform to the Laws of England and of this Province." *

This form was devised as a protection to the province, which the Council considered as possibly " endangered by such numbers of strangers daily poured in, who being ignorant of our Language & Laws, & settling in a body together, make, as it were a distinct people from his Majesties Subjects." The subscription to this oath was required of all Germans coming to Pennsylvania until after 1750. The original lists, giving names of subscribers, the ships in which they were brought, and the dates of arrival, are still preserved at Harrisburg, and have been published in the Pennsylvania *Archives*, 2d Series, vol. xvii. They have also been published by Rupp. These lists contain over thirty thousand names. From the fact that all the subscribers were men, and presumably many of them heads of families, it is safe to conclude that this Palatine immigration brought to the province, by the middle of

* *Penn. Col. Records*, iii., 283.

the eighteenth century, over sixty thousand souls.

This outward flow from the Palatinate was so great that the committee at Rotterdam became alarmed. Their resources for forwarding the people and for caring for them while awaiting shipment were overtaxed, and they endeavored to discourage the spirit of emigration by the most forbidding tales of sorrowful experiences undergone by the emigrants, of which tales the following is a sample :

· " We learn from New York that a ship from Rotterdam, going to Philadelphia with one hundred and fifty Palatines, wandered twenty-four weeks at sea. When they finally arrived at port they were nearly all dead. The rest were forced to subsist on rats and vermin, and were very sick and weak." *

This horrible example, however, did not prove a very powerful deterrent. The stream still kept on.

Notwithstanding the alarm at first felt in the province because of so great importation of foreigners, the value of it to the community was not long in coming to official statement. In 1738 Lieutenant-Governor Thomas, making

* *Penn. Hist. Mag.*, ii., 131.

an address to the Council touching some proposed measures of restriction, used the following most emphatic language :

" This Province has been for some years the Asylum
of the distressed Protestants of the Palatinate and other
parts of Germany, and I believe it may with truth be
said, that the present flourishing condition of it is in a
great measure owing to the Industry of those People;
and should any discouragement divert them from coming hither, it may well be apprehended that the value of
your Lands will fall, and your advance to wealth be much
slower." *

Some years afterwards there were certain out-
croppings of disfavor towards the Palatines,
which seem to have been of a political character.   In 1755 Samuel Wharton published a
pamphlet, in which he expressed great dread
of German preponderance, and represented that
that people were hostile to the government.
" Instead of peaceable, industrious people as
before, they have become insolent, sullen, and
turbulent."   In January of the same year a
bill was introduced into the Council to limit
the importation of Palatines.   The Governor
objected that the measure was inhuman.   The
bill caused great discussion both in the Coun-

* *Penn. Col. Records*, iii., 315.

cil and out of it, and was referred to a committee which presently reported it back with
amendments, and also said, " But, as the difference in sentiment was very great, and on points
which the Assembly were very fond of, it was
thought best to keep the Bill for some time,
lest the Amendments might add to the Heat,
already too great." In the following April—
probably because "the Heat" had lessened—
the bill was taken up and passed. But it was
vetoed by the Governor ;* and that is the last
we read of opposition to the Palatines in Pennsylvania. By their steadiness, industry, frugality, religious habitudes and patriotic devotion
to their new country, they not only established
their own prosperity, but also won their way
to the regard of the province, upon which their
coming had brought unmeasured blessing. Of
such influence and impression most weighty
testimony is borne by no less competent a
judge than Benjamin Franklin,† who, in 1766,
testified before a committee of the British
House of Commons that of the one hundred
and sixty thousand whites in the Province of·

* *Penn. Col. Records*, iv., 225, 345 *et seq.*
† *Penn. Hist. Mag.*, x., 391.

Pennsylvania about one third were Germans,
and described them as "a people who brought
with them the greatest of all wealth,—industry
and integrity, and characters that had been
superpoised and developed by years of suffering and persecution." *

At a much later day, after a hundred years
had shown the fruitage of this Palatine seed,
Judge Pennypacker, himself an offshoot of that
stock, thus wrote :

"No Pennsylvania names are more cherished at home
and more deservedly known abroad than those of Wister,
Shoemaker, Muhlenberg, Weiser, Heister, Keppile, and
Keim, . . . and there are few Pennsylvanians, not comparatively recent arrivals, who cannot be carried back
along some of their ancestral lines to the country of the
Rhine. . . . Pennsylvania is deeply indebted to the
German settlers, who found a home within her borders,
for the rapid advances which she early made towards
prosperity. . . . It is eminently proper that we of
the present day should consider these causes—and the
incentives which prompted these [people] from Switzerland, Alsace, and the Palatinate, whose industry, frugality, and integrity proved so beneficial to the Colony."

Had this address of Judge Pennypacker
been made in still more recent day, he might
have added to his list of Pennsylvania's Pala-

* *Penn. Hist. Mag.*, iv., 3.

tine worthies the names of Zollicoffer, Heintzelman, and Siegel—names of honor among
the soldiers of the Union in the War of the
Rebellion. Worthy to be set also with these
is that of Hartranft—borne by one of the
most efficient governors of the State, and also
by one of the most scholarly divines of the
American Church.

And to these, others of equal honor might
be added. But there is no need. The story
of these Palatine folk in Pennsylvania and in
New York is in itself a sufficient evidence that,
when they came over the sea, they brought
with them qualities and virtues which any land
might be glad to welcome, and that, like men
of other stock,—the Puritan, Dutch, Hugue-
not,—they conferred upon their new country
blessings which it could not afford to lose.

NOTE I.

The following list of names, found in the records of the Palatine Immigrations and still common in the places settled by these people, suggests the sturdy and permanent quality of that stock. This list, be it said, is only fragmentary and suggestive, there being no need of complete transcription of those preserved in the records and archives of New York and Pennsylvania. The most of these names, it will be noted, retain to-day their original form. Any special changes from that form in modern use are noted with their originals :

Becker.

Kelmer, Kilmer.

Wolleben and de Wolleben, Wolven.

Man, Mann.

Kremer, Kromer.

Marterstork, Manterstock.

Froelich, Freligh, Fralick.

Egner.

Richart, Rickard.

Eckertin, Eckard, Eckert.

Emrich, Emerick.

Werner, Warner

Scheerer, Schearer.

Kneiskern, Kniskern.

Hartman.

Conrad.

Christian.

Heiser.

Herttranftt, Hartranft.

Schnell.

Schell.

Nelles, Nellis.

Dachstader, Dochstater.

Meyer, Myer, Myers.
Kuntz.
Dietrich, Dedrick.
Turck.
Mynderse.
Dietz.
Richtmeyer, Rightmyer.
Beller.
Wirtman, Wortman.
Sype.
Bronner.
Albrecht, Allbright.
Lichtner, Lintner.
Aappell, Appell.
Acker.
Bower.
Schurtz.
Muller.
Deichert, Decker.
Hoffman.
Ehle, Ehl, Uhl.*
Jung, Young.
Nehr, Neahr.
Reisch, Rish.
Hager.
Houck.
Bergman.
Weiser.
Angle, Angell.

Bellinger.
Widerwachs, Weatherwax.
Hagedorn.
Schaffer, Schaeffer and
    Schoeffer, Shaver.
Leyer, Lawyer.
Kuhn, Koon, Coon.
Winter.
Linck, Link.
Schneider, Snyder.
Bauch, Bouck.
Kyser, Keiser, Keyser.
Segendorf.
Laux, Loucks.
Fuchs, Fox.
Webber, Weaver.
Bernhard, Bernard.
Arendorff, Allendorph.
Weygandt, Wygant, and
    many other forms.
Christler.
Yeager.
Brunner.
Hess.
Wagner.
Neff.
Funk.
Stickler.
Gertner.

*From this stock in Dutchess Co., N. Y., came Edwin F. Uhl,
U. S. Ambassador to Berlin in 1896-7.

Schiltz, Schultz, Schultis. Gentner.
Wolfe. Schenefeldt, Shufelt.
Schumacher, Schoemaker. Keim.
Schoonmaker. Dillinger.
Baer. Schoup.
W a n n e r m a k e r, Wana- Benker, Banker.
    maker. Sullenger, Sellinger.
Newkirk. Swartz, Swart.
Klein, Cline. Michaells.
Planck, Plank. Kiener, Keener.
Sieknerin, Siekner, Signer. Diebenderf, Devendorf.
Bronck, Brink. Simmierman, Zimmerman.
Wormser. Siegler.
Hayd, Haight, and Hayt. Zollicoffer.
Dill. Timmerman.

This list might be indefinitely prolonged, but it is already sufficient for the purpose of illustration.

NOTE II.

The original Indentures by which Gov. Hunter apprenticed eighty-four of the Palatine children are preserved in the Library of the State of New York, bound together in one volume. They are all alike, save as to dates, names, and sex. Some of them are signed by the Governor as party of the first part, and in others his name is signed without the signature of the master. None of the children, however, was bound to him. Most of the indentures are witnessed by J. S. Wileman, who occupied the office of Register. A specimen is given below. As the Indenture which bound Zenger to Bradford, it has a special interest of its own.

" THIS INDENTURE, made the Twenty Sixth Day of October, *Anno Domini*, 1710, and in the Ninth Year of the Reign of our Sovereign Lady ANNE by the Grace of God of Great Britain, France and Ireland, Queen, Defender of the Faith, &c. Between His Excellency *Robert Hunter*, Esqr ; Capt. General and Governor in Chief of the Provinces of *New York*, *New Jersey*, and Territories depending thereon in *America*, and Vice-Admiral of the same &c., of the one part, And William Bradford of the City of New York Printer, of the other part, Whereas his said Excellency in Council having determined the putting out of the Orphans of the Palatines (and some of those other Children whose Parents have too many to look after them and mind their Labour) for a certain time, upon the Conditions following, (*to wit*) The Boys till they arrive at the Age of Twenty one years, and the Girls till they arrive at the Age of Nineteen years ; The Persons taking them entring into

Indentures, and Bond with Surety, in the Secretary's
Office, to provide them with good and wholesome Meat,
Drink, Lodging and Cloathing, and at the Expiration of
the time to Surrender them to the Government ; his
Excellency and Council engaging they shall respec-
tively Serve till they arrive at the Ages aforesaid. Now
this *Indenture Witnesseth*, That John Peter Zenger of
the Age of Thirteen years, or there-abouts, Son of Han-
nah Zenger Widdow, one of the *Palatines* aforesaid, of
his own free and voluntary Will by the Consent of the
said Mother, and also By the consent and approbation
of his Excellency, hath put himself out to the said William Bradford, his executors and administrators, with him
and them to dwell and serve from the day of the date
hereof for and during and unto the full end and term of
Eight years from thence next ensuing and fully be Com-
pleat and Ended, for all which said Term of Eight years
the said John Peter Zenger the said William Bradford
his executors, and administrators well and truly shall
serve, his and their Commands lawful and honest everywhere he shall do : The Goods of his said master his executors and administrators he shall not waste or destroy,
nor from the Service of his said master his executors or
administrators day nor night shall absent or prolong
himself, but in all things as a good and faithful servant
shall bear and behave himself towards his said master
his executors & administrators during the said Term
aforesaid. And the said William Bradford for himself
his Executors and Administrators and every of them
doth Covenant, Promise and Grant to and with his said
Excellency and his Successors, that the said William
Bradford his executors and administrators shall and

will during all the said Term of Eight years find and
provide for the said John Peter Zenger good, sufficient
and wholesome Meat, Drink and Cloathing; And also
shall and will at the end and Expiration of the said
Term of Eight years surrender and deliver up the said
John Peter Zenger well Cloathed to his said Excellency,
or to the Governour or Commander in Chief of the said
Province of New York, for the time being.

"*In Witness* whereof his said Excellency and the said
William Bradford have hereunto Interchangeably set
their Hands and Seals the day and year first above
Written.

"WILL. BRADFORD. (seal)

"Sealed and Delivered in the Presence of [the several
interlineations aforesaid of ye words, Executors and
Administrators being first Interlined.]

"J. S. WILEMAN."

Tho the form of indenture calls for the signature of
the Governor, yet his name is not affixed to the paper
under which Zenger was bound. A special and curious
clause of the indenture is that which requires the surrender to the Governor of the apprentices, on the expiration of their terms, instead of the usual turning over to
their own mastership and guidance. What the Governor
proposed to do with the young men and women thus
returned to him does not appear, and it is not probable
that he was at any time called upon to take further order about these boys and girls. By the time that their
terms of service had expired his Excellency had quite
given over any paternal care of the Palatines.

NOTE III.

List of the authorities consulted and cited :

Menzel's *History of Germany.*

Lewis' *History of Germany.*

Butler's *Revolutions in Germany.*

Labberton's *Historical Atlas.*

Macaulay's *Essay on the War of the Succession.*

Macaulay's *History of England.*

Mortimer's *History of England.*

Smollett's *History of England.*

Burnet's *History of His Own Time.*

Luttrell's *Diary.*

Learned's *History for Ready Reference.*

Transactions of the Albany Institute, vol. vii. Article by Dr. Homes.

Hawks' *History of North Carolina.*

Martin's *History of North Carolina.*

Williamson's *History of North Carolina.*

Rumple's *Rowan County, N. C.*

Virginia Historical Collections.

Virginia Historical Society Papers.

Campbell's *History of Virginia.*

Cooke's *History of Virginia.*

Magill's *History of Virginia.*

Conway's *Barons of the Potomac.*

Colonial History of the State of New York.

Documentary History of the State of New York. (Quarto edition.)

Lamb's *History of the City of New York.*

Schuyler's *Colonial New York.*

Booth's *History of New York.*

Smith's *History of New York*.

Dunlap's *History of New York*.

Calendar of Land Papers of New York.

Magazine of American History, 1871.

Holmes' *Annals*.

Addison's *Spectator*.

Ruttenber's *History of Orange County, N. Y.*

Ruttenber's *Indian Tribes of Hudson River*.

Smith's *History of Rhinebeck*.

Mellick's *Story of an Old Farm*.

Sims' *History of Schoharie*.

Brown's *Sketch of Schoharie*.

Hopkins' *Historical Memoirs of the Housatunnock Indians*.

Barber and Howe, *Historical Collections*.

Parkman's *Half Century of Conflict*.

Benton's *History of Herkimer County, N. Y.*

Frothingham's *Montgomery County, N. Y.*

Williamson's *History of Maine*.

Barry's *History of Massachusetts*.

Hutchinson's *History of Massachusetts Bay*.

Pennsylvania Colonial Records.

Pennsylvania Historical Magazine.

Pennsylvania Magazine of History.

Rupp's *History of Berks County, Pa.*

C. Z. Weiser's *Life of Conrad Weiser*.

H. A. Muhlenberg's *Life of Gen. Peter Muhlenberg*.

Miss Ayres' *Life of Dr. W. A. Muhlenberg*.

Sachse's *German Pietists of Provincial Pennsylvania*.

Rupp's *Collection of Thirty Thousand Names of Immigrants to Pennsylvania*.

Various Cyclopædias.

INDEX.

Acadians, 257
Adams, Samuel, 139
Adams, Sheriff, abused, 240
Addison, Joseph, 106, 111
Alarm in Pennsylvania, 7, 296–300
Albany, Charity of Dutch in, 213
Albany, Councils at, 242, 262, 263
Albany," "Gentlemen of, 222, 234, 252
Alexander, James, 136, 137
Alsace, 21
Andernach, 40
Anne, Queen, 51, 79, 83
Annsbury, 142
Apprenticing children, 132
Archives at Harrisburg, 295, 298
Arrest of Palatines at Albany, 252
Atrocities of the war, 38
Augsburg, League of, 36
Augustine, 31
Austria, 47
Authorities, 18, Note III

Baden, 21
Bad Faith of Home Government, 146, 177, 183, 189
Barnstaple, 84
Bavaria, 25, 36, 47

Bayard, Col. Nicholas, 68, 115, *note*, 218, 228
Bayard, Samuel, 218–222
Bedford, 84
Beekman, Henry, 206
Bell, Church, 72
Belletre, M. de, 278
Bellomont, Lord, 119, 175, 219
Benton, Judge, 7
Berks County, Pa., 294
Births at Schoharie, 255
Blenheim, Battle of, 48
Block Island, 127
Boston, 224, 247
Bouck, Gov. W. C., 272
Bradford, William, 135
Brandt's raid, 272
Bread and Beer allowance, 166
Bridger, John, 123, 175
Brunnen-dorp, 217
Burgoyne, 47
Burnet, Bishop, 54
Burnett, Gov., 205, 258, 262, 276, 292
Burnetsfield Patent, 275
Byrd, Col. William, 101

Calvin 28
Camps, East and West, 70, 142
Canada Creek, 261
Canajoharie, 261
Cape Fear River, 87

313

Carolina, Settlement in, 86
Casks for tar, 159
Cast, Mr., 150, 159, 168
Certificate refused by Palatines, 244, 245
Chambers Creek, 66
Charles, Elector Palatine, 27, 35
Charles Louis, Elector Pal., 35
Charles II. of Spain, 45
Churches at the Camps, 71, 204, 205
Clarendon, Earl of, 189–191, 227
Clarke, Sec'y, 152, 158, 185, 244
Coble's Kill, The, 217, 231
Codweis, John Conrad, 68
Coeymans, Andries, 234
Colden, Cadwallader, 74, 205, 218
Cologne, 21, 40, 41
Commissioners, English, 83
Commission to England, 245
Complaints at the Manor, 149
Conradus, Octavius, 68
Consistory of N. Y. Dutch Church, 213
Contracts, 90, 116, 155
Cornbury, Lord, 190, 222, note
Cosby, Gov. 135
Court on the Manor, 159
"Cujus regio, ejus religio," 31, 45

Dartmouth, Lord, 189
De Lancey, Ch. Justice, 135
Dellius, Dominie, 239
Departure to Schoharie, 213
Deputies from Schoharie, 245–251
Desertions from the Manor, 163
Dickinson, Jonathan, 296
Disciples of Ephrata, 268
Discontent, 150, 161, 170, 253, 259, 262, 274
Dispersions in England, 81
Dongan, Gov. 66, 144, 192
Dorps at Schoharie, 217

Drachenfels, 40
Dunkers, 268
Du Pré 123, 140
Dutch Church in N. Y., 213

Elizabeth Charlotte, 35
Elizabeth Town, 142
Ephrata, 268, 290
Erghimer, 267
Eugene, Prince, 48
Evans, Capt. John, 66
Expenses on Palatine account, 79, 188

Failure, Causes of, 171
Farrar, 86
"Five Partners," see Partners
Fletcher, Gov. 62, 66, 115, note, 218
Fountaintown, 217
Fox Creek, 211, 217, 231
Franklin, Benjamin, 288, 301
Frederick III. of Zimmern, 26, 29
French and Indian attacks on Mohawk, 278, 279
French War, 152, 289
Fuch's Dorp, 217

Ganendagaren, 261
Garloch's Dorp, 273
Garloch, Elias, 260, 273
Gates, General, 17
Gazette, New York, 136
Genealogy, v
Generosity of England, 13, 79, 92
Geneva, 28
Georgetown, 142
Gerlach, John Christ, 232
German Flats, 277
Germanna, 98, 99
German Patent, 66, 69
Germantown, N. Y., 145, 205
Germantown, Pa., 268
Gibraltar, 49
Glebe, 64, 69, 74
Glebe School House, 72

Governor's Island, 126
Graffenried, Cristopher de, 86
Graffenried, Metcalf de, 98
Grand Alliance, 37
Grants, Fraudulent, 62, 66, 218, 239
Grievances," "Statement of, 161, 225, 237, 242, 243, 246

Hagatorn, Christophel, 205
Hager, Rev. John Fred., 70, 204, 254, 286
Halberstadt, 60
Hamilton, Andrew, 137
Hartman's Dorp, 260
Hartman Vinedecker, 262
Hartranft, 303
Hay, Lady, 111, 122
Haysbury, 142
Heidelberg, 21, 40, 43
Heidelberg Catechism, 30
Heidelberg, Pa., 283
Heintzelman, 303
Helderburg Mts., 211, 213
Henneman, Prof., 102
Herbert Frigate, 127
Herkimer, Nicholas, 17, 267, 277, 279, 280, 281
Herkimer, City of, 277
Herrenberg, 284
Herschias, 71
Historian, Duty of, 5
Holland, 37, 57
Holstein, 63
Homes, Dr. 52, 55, 253
Horses, Return of, 283
House of Commons, Report to, 51, 197–200
Hudson River, 114, 141
Huguenots, 36
Hunter, Gov., 103, 111, 156, 170, 178–187, 242, 244
Huntersfield, 232
Hunter's Resentment, 214, 226, 235, 238, 243, 249, 254
Hunterstown, 142

Ignorance, Charge of, 4, 207, 221, 236, 273
Immigration to New Jersey, 60; of 1709, 63; of 1710, 2, 3, chap. iv.; of 1717 to Pennsylvania, 264; of religionists to Penna., 268; character of, 10; causes of, chap. ii., 75; volume of, 7, 76, 84, 265, 294–298
Indentures of children, 132, Note II
Indian Councils at Albany, 242, 262
Indian Embassy to England, 104
Indian Gift of Schoharie, 107, 115, 131, 212, 228
Indians of Carolina, 96
Influence of Palatines, 5, 15, 299, 301
Ingoldsby, Col., 165
Ingoldsby, Lt. Gov., 67
Ireland, Settlement in, 85
Iron mines in Virginia, 100

James II. of England, 37, 47
Johnson, Guy, 280, 281
Johnson, Sir William, 280
John William, Elector Palatine, 27, 44, 55, 59, 297
Journal, New York Weekly, 136
Julich, 41
Justices, Palatine, 129

Kaatsbaan, 143
Kalm, Peter, 295
Karigondonte, 209
Keith, Sir William, 263, 281
Kelpius, 268
Kidd, Captain, 193
Kill, Roeloff Jansen's, 144
"King of the Palatines," 95
Kingsbury, 204
Kingston, Justices of, 163
Kniskern's Dorp, 217
Kockerthal, 61, 65, 70, 130, 254
Kohl, 86

Kreuznach, 40
Kuckheim, 40

Labadists, 268
Land agents in Palatinate, 51, 53, 56
Land Grants, Extravagant, 62, 66, 218, 239; at Schoharie, 228–235; on the Mohawk, 239, 260, 261, 275, 282
Land troubles at Schoharie, 218, 239
Lawson, John, 95
Lawyer's Purchase, 235
Lebanon County, Pa., 294
Legend of Palatine Light, 127
Leisler, 184, 192
Leopold, Emperor, 42, 46
List-masters, 160
Livingston Manor, 143, 194, 205, 206
Livingston, Robert, 134, 141, 159, 166, 189, 190–196, 205, 227
Livingston, Robert, Jr., 193, 221
Logan, James, 296
London, Palatines in, 76
Long Island, 127
Lorraine, 21
Louis the Severe, 26
Louis XIV., 34
Lovelace, Lord, 62, 69, 110, 120
Lutheran Church in N. Y., 144
Lutheranism in the Palatinate, 28
Lyon, Ship, 126

Macaulay, 4, 39
Maintenon, Mad. de, 36, 38
Mainz, 21
Manisees Island, 127
Mannheim, 21, 40, 41
Mannheim, N. Y., 277
Marlborough, 48
Melac, 39
Mennonites in Pennsylvania, 268
Michell, Lewis, 86, 94

Middleburgh, N. Y., 210, 222, 217, 272
Middle Line of Palatinate, 26
Migration from Newburgh, 73
Miller, Rev. John Peter, 290
Misunderstandings, 1, 50, 236
Mohawk River, 114, 122, 260; Fall of, 140; German names on, 277; Settlement on, 272, 277–281
Money, Failure of, 164, 169, 170, 177–183, 244
Montclas, 38, 49
Moravians, 268
Morris Jr., Lewis, 234
Mortality at sea, 125; in first year, 145
Muhlenberg, Frederick, 290
Muhlenberg, Henry Melchior, 17, 286, 290–292
Muhlenberg, Peter, 291
Muhlenberg, William A., 291
Munster, 86
Murmurs of London poor, 197, 199
Murphy, the Indian fighter, 272
Mutiny on the Manor, 150

Name-Lists, vi., vii., 265, Note I.
Nantes, Edict of, 36, 38
Naturalization Act, 52, 63, 197–200
Naval Stores, 62, 109, 114, 116, 118, 140, 142, 146, 158, 165, 171–175, 191, 201–203
Neuburg, House of, 27, 66
Neuse River, 87, 93, 95
New Berne, 93
Newborn, 268
Newburgh, 66, 74
New Forest of Hampshire, 83
New Foundland fisheries, 84
Newington, Parish of, 80
New Jersey, Settlement in, 60, 268
Newkirk, 277

New Village, 142
New York, Avoidance of, 295
New York, Influence of Palatines on, 16, 74, 146, 207, 271, 277
Nicholson, Col., 104, 155
Number of Palatines in 1718, 250-255
Nutten Island, 126, 129, 131, 267

Oath subscribed by Palatines, 297
Ober-Weiser's Dorp, 229
Old Stone Church at Schoharie, 218, 272
Olevian, 29
Oppenheim, N. Y., 277
Oppression in America, 14, chaps. v., vi.
Oriskany, Battle of 16, 281
Otho, Count Palatine, 26
Oudenarde, Battle of, 48

Palatinate, Division of, 26 ; Origin of name, 22
Palatine, Bridge, 277 ; Town of, 277 ; Count, 22 ; Count, in England, 23 ; in Hungary, 23 ; Elector, 26 ; Light and Ship, Legend of, 127 ; Houses, 80 ; Parish by Quassaic, 69, 74 ; Poem of The, 128
Palatines in French and Indian War 277, 278 , in Revolution, 280, 281
Partners," "Five, 222, 239, 241, 252 ; Seven, 234
Patents at Schoharie, 228-235
Pennsylvania, Influence of Palatines on, 12, 299-303
Pennsylvania, Migration to, 73, 263, 269-271, 281, 284, 293
Pennypacker, Judge, 302
Pfalz, The, 21
Philadelphia, 60, 266
Philip of Anjou, 47, 49
Philip of Orleans, 35

Philip V. of Spain, 47
Philip William, 27, 40, 44
Philippsberg, 40
Philipse, Justice, 135
Pietists, 268
Pine, see Naval Stores
Pine, varieties of, 173
Pirates, 247
Pitch, see Naval Stores
Political foresight, 139
Politics, Relation to English, 196
Pollock, Thomas, 98
Poor of London, Murmurs of, 197, 199
Popple, Sec'y, 182, 187, 258
Poverty of immigrants, 3, 77, 295
Premium on Naval Stores, 116, 120, 191
Press, Freedom of the, 5, 135-139
Prussia, 47
Punishments on the Manor, 160
Purchase at Schoharie, 210, 225

Quagnant, Chief, 285
Quassaick, 66
Quebec, 279
Queensbury, 142
Quit-rents, 230

Ramillies, Battle of, 48
Ratisbon, Diet of, 42
Redemptioner, 287, 295
Reformed Church at German-town, N. Y., 205
Religious, liberty, 12, 31 ; sects in Pennsylvania, 268 ; troubles in the Palatinate, 27-33, 55
Restrictive legislation, 9, 59, 297-301
Revolution, Palatines in the, 16, 280, 281
Rhine, The, 21, 34, 41
Rhinebeck, 207 ; History of, 228
Roman Catholics among the emigrants, 82 ; in Pennsylvania, petition to disarm, 289

Rotterdam, Committee at, 57, 76, 266, 299
Rozin, *see* Naval Stores
Rudolf and Rudolphine Line of the Palatinate, 26
Ruins on the Rhine, 41
Rupp, vi., 298
Ryswick, Peace of, 43

Sackett, Richard, 158, 159
"Sallary" for Kockerthal, 63
Sassouan, Chief, 271, 293
Saugerties, 142, 145
Sawyer's Creek, 141
Scheff, 246, 250
Schemes for settlement, 83
Schenectady, 218, 241
Schoharie, 107, 108, 115, 132, 140, 149, 154, 156, 169, 208, 211, 216, 218, 239, 250, 271–273
Schuyler, John, 221
Schuyler, Myndert, 221
Schuyler, Peter, 104
Schuyler, Philip, 232, 234
Schwenkfelders, 268
"Servants to the Crown," 114, 117, 149, 161
"Seven Partners," 234
Seventh-Day Baptists of Ephrata, 290
Sharpe, Jacob, 205
Shenandoah Valley, 101
Sheriff of Albany, 240
Shoemaker, Jacob, 205
Shute, Governor, 177
Siegel, General, 303
Simmeren, *see* Zimmern
Sims, J. R., 220, 283
Smith, E. M., 228
Smith, Lawrence, 166
Smith, William, 136, 137
Soldiers on the Manor, 160, 165
Soldiers, Palatine, 280
Sources of information, 18
Spanish Succession, 46–50
Spectator, The, 106

"Speculation, Objects of," 11, 51
Spires, 21, 40, 41
Spotswood, Governor, 99
Staats, Samuel, 231, 232
St. Germain, 37, 47
St. Leger, 17, 28
St. Olaves, 199
Strasburg, Va., 101
Subsistence, Contract for, 166
Sufferings, at Newburgh, 67 ; in Schoharie, 216 ; on the Manor, 149, 161
Suspension of work, 163
Susquehanna River, 283
Swabia, 53
Swatara River, 281, 283, 293
Swiss Colonists, 89

Tar, *see* Naval stores
Tattler, The, 106
Thankskamir, 66
Thomas, Lt. Gov., 297
Treves, 21, 38, 41
Tulpehocken, The, 270, 283, 293
Turenne, 35
Turpentine, *see* Naval Stores
Tuscaroras, 96

Ursinus, 29
Utrecht, Peace of, 48

Van Brugh, Peter, 221
Van Dam, Rip, 231, 232, 234
Van Rensselaer, Rev. Nicholas, 192
Versailles, 37
Villages in Schoharie, 217 ; on the Hudson, 142
Villars, Marshall, 49
Vinedecker, Hartman, 262, 282
Violence at Schoharie, 241, 253
Virginia, Settlement in, 99
Volume of immigration, 7, 76, 84, 265, 294–298

Volunteers, Palatine, 145, 153, 157
Vroman, Adam, 222–225
Vroman Patent, 229
Vroman's Nose, 223

Wahl, Edward, 280
Walpole, 244
Walrath, 246
War of the Grand Alliance, 34; of Spanish Succession, 45–50
Weiser, Conrad, 17, 75, 76, 124, 224, 225, 252, 259, 262, 282, 284–293
Weiser, John Conrad, 130, 131, 134, 153, 160, 224, 240, 242, 246–251, 292
Weiser's Dorp, 217, 229, 240
Wharton's pamphlet against the Palatines, 300
Whittier, 128
Wileman, Henry, 221
Wileman, J. S., 306
William the Silent, 32

William III. of England, 37, 42, 43, 47
Winchenbach, 71
Wine culture, 110
Wissahickon, 268
Wittenberg, 28
Wolfenbuttel, 60
Wolven, Godfried De, 233
Womelsdorf, 287
Women, Palatine, 241
Woollen manufacture, 115, 118
Worms, 21
Wurtemburg, 21, 42

York, Lewis, 233
York, William, 233

Zeh, Magdalena, 241
Zeiher, Herr, 44
Zenger, John Peter, 135–139, Note II
Zimmern Line of the Palatinate, 26, 27
Zollicoffer, General, 303

The Story of the Nations.

MESSRS. G. P. PUTNAM'S SONS take pleasure in announcing that they have in course of publication, in co-operation with Mr. T. Fisher Unwin, of London, a series of historical studies, intended to present in a graphic manner the stories of the different nations that have attained prominence in history.

In the story form the current of each national life is distinctly indicated, and its picturesque and noteworthy periods and episodes are presented for the reader in their philosophical relation to each other as well as to universal history.

It is the plan of the writers of the different volumes to enter into the real life of the peoples, and to bring them before the reader as they actually lived, labored, and struggled—as they studied and wrote, and as they amused themselves. In carrying out this plan, the myths, with which the history of all lands begins, will not be overlooked, though these will be carefully distinguished from the actual history, so far as the labors of the accepted historical authorities have resulted in definite conclusions.

The subjects of the different volumes have been planned to cover connecting and, as far as possible, consecutive epochs or periods, so that the set when completed will present in a comprehensive narrative the chief events in the great STORY OF THE NATIONS; but it is, of course, not always practicable to issue the several volumes in their chronological order.

The "Stories" are printed in good readable type, and in handsome 12mo form. They are adequately illustrated and furnished with maps and indexes. Price, per vol., cloth, $1.50. Half morocco, gilt top, $1.75.

The following are now ready:

GREECE. Prof. Jas. A. Harrison.
ROME. Arthur Gilman.
THE JEWS. Prof. James K. Hosmer.
CHALDEA. Z. A. Ragozin.
GERMANY. S. Baring-Gould.
NORWAY. Hjalmar H. Boyesen.
SPAIN. Rev. E. E. and Susan Hale.
HUNGARY. Prof. A. Vámbéry.
CARTHAGE. Prof. Alfred J. Church.
THE SARACENS. Arthur Gilman.
THE MOORS IN SPAIN. Stanley Lane-Poole.
THE NORMANS. Sarah Orne Jewett.
PERSIA. S. G. W. Benjamin.
ANCIENT EGYPT. Prof. Geo. Rawlinson.
ALEXANDER'S EMPIRE. Prof. J. P. Mahaffy.
ASSYRIA. Z. A. Ragozin.
THE GOTHS. Henry Bradley.
IRELAND. Hon. Emily Lawless.
TURKEY. Stanley Lane-Poole.
MEDIA, BABYLON, AND PERSIA. Z. A. Ragozin.
MEDIÆVAL FRANCE. Prof. Gustave Masson.
HOLLAND. Prof. J. Thorold Rogers.
MEXICO. Susan Hale.
PHŒNICIA. Geo. Rawlinson.

THE HANSA TOWNS. Helen Zimmern.
EARLY BRITAIN. Prof. Alfred J. Church.
THE BARBARY CORSAIRS. Stanley Lane-Poole.
RUSSIA. W. R. Morfill.
THE JEWS UNDER ROME. W. D. Morrison.
SCOTLAND. John Mackintosh.
SWITZERLAND. R. Stead and Mrs. A. Hug.
PORTUGAL. H. Morse Stevens.
THE BYZANTINE EMPIRE. C. W. C. Oman.
SICILY. E. A. Freeman.
THE TUSCAN REPUBLICS. Bella Duffy.
POLAND. W. R. Morfill.
PARTHIA. Geo. Rawlinson.
JAPAN. David Murray.
THE CHRISTIAN RECOVERY OF SPAIN. H. E. Watts.
AUSTRALASIA. Greville Tregarthen.
SOUTHERN AFRICA. Geo. M. Theal.
VENICE. Alethea Wiel.
THE CRUSADES. T. S. Archer and C. L. Kingsford.
VEDIC INDIA. Z. A. Ragozin.
BOHEMIA. C. E. Maurice.
CANADA. J. G. Bourinot.
THE BALKAN STATES. William Miller.
BRITISH RULE IN INDIA. R. W. Frazer.

CPSIA information can be obtained
at www.ICGtesting.com
Printed in the USA
BVHW041346040821
613439BV00003B/188

9 781375 653824